Human Language Technologies: The 2010 Annual Conference of the North American Chapter of the Association for Computational Linguistics (NAACL HLT 2010)

Student Research Workshop

Los Angeles, California, USA
2 June 2010

ISBN: 978-1-61738-707-4

Printed from e-media with permission by:

Curran Associates, Inc.
57 Morehouse Lane
Red Hook, NY 12571

CURRAN ASSOCIATES INC. proceedings .com

Some format issues inherent in the e-media version may also appear in this print version.

Printed by Curran Associates, Inc. (2010)

For permission requests, please contact the Association for Computational Linguistics
at the address below.

Association for Computational Linguistics
209 N. Eighth Street
Stroudsburg, Pennsylvania 18360

Phone: 1-570-476-8006
Fax: 1-570-476-0860

acl@aclweb.org

Additional copies of this publication are available from:

Curran Associates, Inc.
57 Morehouse Lane
Red Hook, NY 12571 USA
Phone: 845-758-0400
Fax: 845-758-2634
Email: curran@proceedings.com
Web: www.proceedings.com

Introduction

Welcome to the 2010 NAACL-HLT Student Research Workshop in Los Angeles, California! The purpose of this workshop is to provide feedback to students whose work may be in its early stages and to help prepare these students to future academic and professional pursuits. During this workshop, each presentation will be followed by a discussion on the work by a panel of senior researchers.

This year, we received 20 submissions from 5 countries. We thank all authors who submitted. We are grateful to the program committee for their time, effort, and professional consideration. We also thank the panelists in advance for their time and helpful feedback. We also owe a debt of gratitude to the 2010 NAACL-HLT main conference organizers and to the National Science Foundation whose support makes many aspects of this workshop possible.

Organizers:

Adriane Boyd, The Ohio State University
Mahesh Joshi, Carnegie Mellon University
Frank Rudzicz, University of Toronto

Faculty Advisors:

Julia Hockenmaier, University of Illinois
Diane Litman, University of Pittsburgh

Program Committee:

Hua Ai, Carnegie Mellon University
Abhishek Arun, University of Edinburgh
Srinivas Bangalore, AT&T
S.R.K. Branavan, Massachusetts Institute of Technology
Chris Brew, The Ohio State University
Chris Callison-Burch, Johns Hopkins University
Nathaneal Chambers, Stanford University
Steve DeNeefe, Information Sciences Institute
Markus Dickinson, Indiana University
Micha Elsner, Brown University
Jenny Finkel, Stanford University
Eric Fosler-Lussier, The Ohio State University
Timothy Fowler, University of Toronto
Oana Frunza, University of Ottawa
Roxana Girju, University of Illinois at Urbana-Champaign
Dan Goldwasser, University of Illinois at Urbana-Champaign
Mark Hasegawa-Johnson, University of Illinois at Urbana-Champaign
Sandra Kuebler, Indiana University
Yang Liu, The University of Texas at Dallas
Daniel Marcu, Information Sciences Institute
Jon May, Information Sciences Institute
Cosmin Munteanu, University of Toronto
Douglas O'Shaughnessy, Institut national de la recherche scientifique
Ted Pedersen, University of Minnesota
Rashmi Prasad, University of Pennsylvania
Partha Pratim Talukdar, University of Pennsylvania
Owen Rambow, Columbia University
Sujith Ravi, Information Sciences Institute
Hannah Rohde, Northwestern University
William Schuler, The Ohio State University
Matthew Stone, Rutgers University
Marilyn Walker, University of California, Santa Cruz
Xiaodan Zhu, University of Toronto

Table of Contents

Workshop Program

Wednesday, June 2, 2010

Session 1

10:40–11:10 *Improving Syntactic Coordination Resolution using Language Modeling*
Philip Ogren

11:10–11:40 *On Automated Evaluation of Readability of Summaries: Capturing Grammaticality, Focus, Structure and Coherence*
Ravikiran Vadlapudi and Rahul Katragadda

11:40–12:10 *Detecting Novelty in the context of Progressive Summarization*
Praveen Bysani

12:10–2:00 **Lunch**

Session 2

2:00–2:30 *Extrinsic Parse Selection*
David Goss-Grubbs

2:30–3:00 *Towards a Matrix-based Distributional Model of Meaning*
Eugenie Giesbrecht

3:00–3:30 *Distinguishing Use and Mention in Natural Language*
Shomir Wilson

6:30–8:30 **Poster Session**

A Learning-based Sampling Approach to Extractive Summarization
Vishal Juneja, Sebastian Germesin and Thomas Kleinbauer

Temporal Relation Identification with Endpoints
Chong Min Lee

Identifying Opinion Holders and Targets with Dependency Parser in Chinese News Texts
Bin Lu

Wednesday, June 2, 2010 (continued)

A Data Mining Approach to Learn Reorder Rules for SMT
Avinesh PVS

Fine-Tuning in Brazilian Portuguese-English Statistical Transfer Machine Translation: Verbal Tenses
Lucia Silva

Note: The following posters were also given as oral presentations.

Improving Syntactic Coordination Resolution using Language Modeling
Philip Ogren

On Automated Evaluation of Readability of Summaries: Capturing Grammaticality, Focus, Structure and Coherence
Ravikiran Vadlapudi and Rahul Katragadda

Extrinsic Parse Selection
David Goss-Grubbs

Towards a Matrix-based Distributional Model of Meaning
Eugenie Giesbrecht

Distinguishing Use and Mention in Natural Language
Shomir Wilson

Improving Syntactic Coordination Resolution Using Language Modeling

Philip V. Ogren
Center for Computational Pharmacology
University of Colorado Denver
12801 E. 17th Ave
Aurora, CO 80045, USA
philip@ogren.info

Abstract

Determining the correct structure of coordinating conjunctions and the syntactic constituents that they coordinate is a difficult task. This subtask of syntactic parsing is explored here for biomedical scientific literature. In particular, the intuition that sentences containing coordinating conjunctions can often be rephrased as two or more smaller sentences derived from the coordination structure is exploited. Generating candidate sentences corresponding to different possible coordination structures and comparing them with a language model is employed to help determine which coordination structure is best. This strategy is used to augment a simple baseline system for coordination resolution which outperforms both the baseline system and a constituent parser on the same task.

1 Introduction

For this work, coordination resolution (CR) refers to the task of automatically identifying the correct coordination structure of coordinating conjunctions. In this study the conjunctions *and* and *or* and the conjuncts they coordinate are examined. CR is an important subtask of syntactic parsing in the biomedical domain because many information extraction tasks require correct syntactic structures to perform well, in particular coordination structures. For example, (Cohen et al., 2009) showed that using a constituent parser trained on biomedical data to provide coordination structures to a high-precision protein-protein interaction recognition system resulted in a significant performance boost from an overall F-measure of 24.7 to 27.6. Coordination structures are the source of a disproportionate number of parsing errors for both constituent parsers (Clegg and Shepherd, 2007) and dependency parsers (Nivre and McDonald, 2008).

CR is difficult for a variety of reasons related to the linguistic complexity of the phenomenon. There are a number of measurable characteristics of coordination structures that support this claim including the following: constituent types of conjuncts, number of words per conjunct, number of conjuncts per conjunction, and the number of conjunctions that are nested inside the conjunct of another conjunction, among others. Each of these metrics reveal wide variability of coordination structures. For example, roughly half of all conjuncts consist of one or two words while the other half consist of three or more words including 15% of all conjuncts that have ten or more words. There is also an increased prevalence of coordinating conjunctions in biomedical literature when compared with newswire text. Table 1 lists three corpora in the biomedical domain that are annotated with deep syntactic structures; CRAFT (described below), GENIA (Tateisi et al., 2005), and Penn BIOIE (Bies et al., 2005). The number of coordinating conjunctions they contain as a percentage of the number of total tokens in each corpus are compared with the Penn Treebank corpus (Marcus et al., 1994). The salient result from this table is that there are 50% more conjunctions in biomedical scientific text than in newswire text. It is also interesting to note that 15.4% of conjunctions in the biomedical corpora are nested inside a conjunct of another con-

Proceedings of the NAACL HLT 2010 Student Research Workshop, pages 1–6,
Los Angeles, California, June 2010.

junction as compared with 10.9% for newswire.

Table 1: Biomedical corpora that provide coordination structures compared with the Penn Treebank corpus.

Corpus	Tokens	Conjunctions	
CRAFT	246,008	7,115	2.89%
GENIA	490,970	14,854	3.03%
BIOIE	188,341	5,036	2.67%
subtotal	925,319	27,005	**2.92%**
PTB	1,173,766	22,888	**1.95%**

The Colorado Richly Annotated Full-Text (CRAFT) Corpus being developed at the University of Colorado Denver was used for this work. Currently, the corpus consists of 97 full-text open-access scientific articles that have been annotated by the Mouse Genome Institute[1] with concepts from the Gene Ontology[2] and Mammalian Phenotype Ontology[3]. Thirty-six of the articles have been annotated with deep syntactic structures similar to that of the Penn Treebank corpus described in (Marcus et al., 1994). As this is a work in progress, eight of the articles have been set aside for a final holdout evaluation and results for these articles are not reported here. In addition to the standard treebank annotation, the *NML* tag discussed in (Bies et al., 2005) and (Vadas and Curran, 2007) which marks nominal subconstituents which do not observe the right-branching structure common to many (but not all) noun phrases is annotated. This is of particular importance for coordinated noun phrases because it provides an unambiguous representation of the correct coordination structure. The coordination instances in the CRAFT data were converted to simplified coordination structures consisting of conjunctions and their conjuncts using a script that cleanly translates the vast majority of coordination structures.

2 Related Work

There are two main approaches to CR. The first approach considers CR as a task in its own right where the solutions are built specifically to perform CR. Often the task is narrowly defined, e.g. only coordinations of the pattern *noun-1 conjunction noun-2 noun-3* are considered, and relies on small training and testing data sets. Generally, such research efforts do not attempt to compare their results with previous results other than in the broadest and most-qualified way. Studies by (Chantree et al., 2005), (Nakov and Hearst, 2005), and (Resnik, 1999) are representative examples of such work. A study by (Shimbo and Hara, 2007) performed CR on sentences from the GENIA corpus containing one instance of the word "and" coordinating noun phrases. They used a sequence alignment algorithm modified for CR drawing on the intuition that conjuncts have similar syntactic constructs. In each of these studies, promising results were achieved by careful application of their respective approaches. However, each study is limited in important respects because they narrowly constrain the problem, use limited training data, and make certain unrealistic assumptions in their experimental setup that make general application of their solutions problematic. For example, in the study by (Shimbo and Hara, 2007) they chose only sentences that have one instance of "and" because their algorithm does not handle nested conjunctions. Additionally, they assume an oracle that provides the system with only sentences that contain coordinated noun phrases.

The work most similar to this study was done by (Hara et al., 2009) in that they define the CR task essentially the same as is done here. Their approach involves a grammar tailored for coordination structures that is coupled with a sequence alignment algorithm that uses perceptrons for learning feature weights of an edit graph. The evaluation metric they use is slightly less strict than the metric used for this study in that they require identification of the left boundary of the left-most conjunct and the right boundary of the right-most conjunct to be counted correct. Two other important differences are that the evaluation data comes from the GENIA corpus and they use gold-standard part-of-speech tags for the input data. Regardless of these relatively minor differences, their performance of 61.5 F-measure far outperforms what is reported below and experiments that are directly comparable to their work will be performed.

[1] `http://www.informatics.jax.org/`

[2] `http://geneontology.org/`

[3] `http://www.informatics.jax.org/searches/MP_form.shtml`

The second main approach considers CR within the broader task of syntactic parsing. Any syntactic parser that generates constituents or dependencies must necessarily perform CR to perform well. Typically, a syntactic parser will have a single, central algorithm that is used to determine all constituents or dependencies. However, this does not preclude parsers from giving special attention to CR by adding CR-specific rules and features. For example, (Nilsson et al., 2006) show that for dependency parsing it is useful to transform dependency structures that make conjunctions the head of their conjuncts into structures in which coordination dependencies are chained. (Charniak and Johnson, 2005) discusses a constituent-based parser that adds two features to the learning model that directly address coordination. The first measures parallelism in the labels of the conjunct constituents and their children and the second measures the lengths of the conjunct constituents. The work done by (Hogan, 2007) focuses directly on coordination of noun phrases in the context of the Collins parser (Collins, 2003) by building a right conjunct using features from the already built left conjunct.

3 Using a Language Model

Consider the following sentence:

> Tyr mutation results in *increased IOP* and *altered diurnal changes*.

By exploiting the coordination structure we can rephrase this sentence as two separate sentences:

- Tyr mutation results in *increased IOP*.
- Tyr mutation results in *altered diurnal changes*.

Using this simple rewrite strategy a candidate sentence for each possible conjunct can be composed. For this sentence there are six possible left conjuncts corresponding to each word to the left of the conjunction. For example, the candidate conjunct corresponding to the third word is *results in increased IOP* and the corresponding sentence rewrite is *Tyr mutation altered diurnal changes*. The resulting candidate sentences can be compared by calculating a sentence probability using a language model. Ideally, the candidate sentence corresponding to the correct conjunct boundary will have a higher probability than the other candidate sentences. One problem with this approach is that the candidate sentences are different lengths. This has a large and undesirable (for this task) impact on the probability calculation. A simple and effective way to normalize for sentence length is by adding[4] the probability of the candidate conjunct (also computed by using the language model) to the probability of the candidate sentence. The probability of each candidate is calculated using this simple metric and then rank ordered. Because the number of candidate conjuncts varies from one sentence to the next (as determined by the token index of the conjunction) it is useful to translate the rank into a percentile. The rank percentile of the candidate conjuncts will be applied to the task of CR as described below. However, it is informative to directly evaluate how good the rank percentile scores of the correct conjuncts are.

To build a language model a corpus of more than 80,000 full-text open-access scientific articles were obtained from PubMed Central[5]. The articles are provided in a simple XML format which was parsed to produce plain text documents using only sections of the articles containing contentful prose (i.e. by excluding sections such as e.g. *acknowledgments* and *references*.) The plain text documents were automatically sentence segmented, tokenized, and part-of-speech tagged resulting in nearly 13 million sentences and over 250 million tagged words. A language model was then built using this data with the SRILM toolkit described in (Stolcke, 2002). Default options were used for creating the language model except that the order of the model was set to four and the "-tagged" option was used. Thus, a 4-gram model with Good-Turing discounting and Katz backoff for smoothing was built.

For each token to the left of a conjunction a candidate conjunct/sentence pair is derived, its probability calculated, and a rank percentile score is assigned to it relative to the other candidates. Because multiple conjuncts can appear on the left-hand-side of the conjunction, the left border of the leftmost conjunct is considered here. The same is done for tokens

[4] logprobs are used here

[5] `http://www.ncbi.nlm.nih.gov/pmc/about/ftp.html`. The corpus was downloaded in September of 2008.

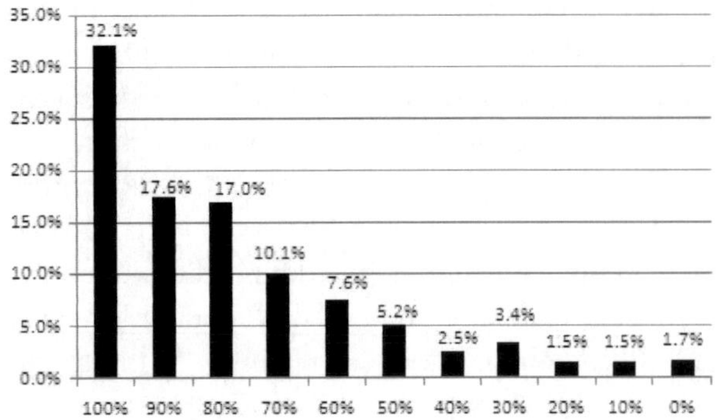

Figure 1: The first column can be read as "The correct conjunct candidate had the highest rank percentile 32.1% of the time." The second column can be read as "The correct conjunct candidate had a rank percentile of 90% or greater 17.6% of the time." The columns add to one.

on the right-hand-side of the conjunction. Figure 1 shows a histogram of the rank percentile scores for the correct left conjunct. The height of the bars correspond to the percentage of the total number of conjunctions in which the correct candidate was ranked within the percentile range. Thus, the columns add to one and generalizations can be made by adding the columns together. For example, 66.7% of the conjunctions (by adding the first three columns) fall above the eightieth percentile. The overall average rank percentage for all of the left-hand-side conjuncts was 81.1%. The median number of candidates on the left-hand-side is 17 (i.e. the median token index of the conjunction is 17). Similar results were obtained for the right-hand-side data but were withheld for space considerations. The overall average rank percentage for right-hand-side conjuncts was 82.2%. This slightly better result is likely due to the smaller median number of candidates on the right-hand-side of 12 (i.e. the median token index of the conjunction is 12 from the end of the sentence.) These data suggest that the rank percentile of the candidate conjuncts calculated in this way could be an effective feature to use for CR.

4 Coordination Resolution

Table 2 reports the performance of two CR systems that are described below. Results are reported as F-Measure at both the conjunct and conjunction levels where a true positive requires all boundaries to be exact. That is, for conjunct level evaluation a conjunct generated by the system must have exactly the same extent (i.e. character offsets) as the conjunct in the gold-standard data in addition to being attached to the same conjunction. Similarly, at the conjunction level a true positive requires that a coordination structure generated by the system has the same number of conjuncts each with extents exactly the same as the corresponding conjunct in the gold-standard coordination structure. Where 10-fold cross-validation is performed, training is performed on roughly 90% of the data and testing on the remaining 10% with the results micro-averaged. Here, the folds are split at the document level to avoid the unfair advantage of training and testing on different sections of the same document.

Table 2: Coordination resolution results at the conjunct and conjunction levels as F-Measure.

	Conjunct	Conjunction
OpenNLP + PTB	55.46	36.56
OpenNLP + CRAFT	58.87	39.50
baseline	59.75	40.99
baseline + LM	**64.64**	**46.40**

The first system performs CR within the broader task of syntactic parsing. Here the constituent parser from the OpenNLP project[6] is applied. This parser was chosen because of its availability and ease of use for both training and execution. It has also been shown by (Buyko et al., 2006) to perform well on biomedical data. The output of the parser is processed by the same conversion script described above. The parser was trained and evaluated on both the Penn Treebank and CRAFT corpora. For the latter, 10-fold cross-validation was performed. Preliminary experiments that attempted to add additional training data from the GENIA and Penn BIOIE corpora proved to be slightly detrimental to performance in both cases. Table 2 shows that CR improves at the conjunction level by nearly three points (from 36.56 to 39.50) by simply training on biomedical data rather than using a model trained on newswire.

The second system that performs CR as a separate

[6]http://opennlp.sf.net

task by using token-level classification to determine conjunct boundaries is introduced and evaluated. In brief, each token to the left of a conjunction is classified as being either a left-hand border of a conjunct for that conjunction or not. Similarly, tokens to the right of a conjunction are classified as either a right-hand border of a conjunct or not. From these token-level classifications and some simple assumptions about the right-hand and left-hand borders of left and right conjuncts, respectively,[7] a complete coordination structure can be constructed. The classifier used was SVM^{light} described in (Joachims, 1999) using a linear kernel. The baseline system uses a number of shallow lexical features (many common to named entity recognition systems) including part-of-speech tags, word and character n-grams, the distance between the focus token and the conjunction, and word-level features such as whether the token is a number or contains a hyphen. A more detailed description of the baseline system is avoided here as this remains a major focus of current and future research efforts and the final system will likely change considerably. Table 2 shows the results of 10-fold cross-validation for the baseline system. This simple baseline system performs at 40.99 F-measure at the conjunction level which is modestly better than the syntactic parser trained on CRAFT.

The baseline system as described above was augmented using the language modeling approach described in Section 3 by adding a simple feature to each token being classified whose value is the rank percentile of the probability of the corresponding conjunct candidate. Again, 10-fold cross-validation was performed. Table 2 shows that this augmented baseline system performs at 46.40 F-measure at the conjunction level which out-performs the baseline system and the CRAFT-trained parser by 5.4 and 6.9 points, respectively. This increase in performance demonstrates that a language model can be effectively purposed for CR.

While the use of a language model to improve CR results is promising, the results in Table 2 also speak to how difficult this task is for machines to perform. In contrast, the task is comparatively easy for humans to perform consistently. To calculate inter-annotator agreement on the CR task, 500 sentences containing either the word "and" or "or" were randomly chosen from the 13 million sentence corpus described in Section 3 and annotated with coordination structures by two individuals, the author and another computer scientist with background in biology. Our positive specific agreement[8] was 91.93 and 83.88 at the conjunct and conjunction level, respectively, for 732 conjunctions. This represents a dramatic gulf between system and human performance on this task but also suggests that large improvements for automated CR should be expected.

5 Future Work

There is much that can be done to move this work forward. Creating comparable results to the study discussed in Section 2 by (Hara et al., 2009) is a top priority. As alluded to earlier, there is much that can be done to improve the baseline system. For example, constraining coordination structures to not overlap except where one is completely nested within the conjunct of another should be enforced as partially overlapping coordination structures never occur in the training data. Similarly, a conjunction that appears inside parentheses should have a coordination structure that is completely contained inside the parentheses. Thorough error analysis should also be performed. For example, it would be interesting to characterize the conjuncts that have a low rank percentile for their calculated probability. Also, it would be useful to measure performance across a number of metrics such as phrase type of the conjuncts, length of conjuncts, whether a coordination structure is nested inside another, etc. Demonstrating that CR can improve syntactic parsing performance and improve the performance of an information extraction system would give this work greater significance.

Conclusion

This work has demonstrated that a language model can be used to improve performance of a simple CR system. This is due to the high rank percentile of the probability of the correct conjunct compared with other possible conjuncts.

[7]For example, the left-hand border of the conjunct to the right of a conjunction will always be the first word following the conjunction.

[8]This measure is directly comparable with F-measure.

References

Ann Bies, Seth Kulick, and Mark Mandel. 2005. Parallel entity and treebank annotation. In *CorpusAnno '05: Proceedings of the Workshop on Frontiers in Corpus Annotations II*, pages 21–28, Morristown, NJ, USA. Association for Computational Linguistics.

Ekaterina Buyko, Joachim Wermter, Michael Poprat, and Udo Hahn. 2006. Automatically adapting an NLP core engine to the biology domain. In *Proceedings of the Joint BioLINK-Bio-Ontologies Meeting. A Joint Meeting of the ISMB Special Interest Group on Bio-Ontologies and the BioLINK Special Interest Group on Text Data M ining in Association with ISMB*, pages 65–68. Citeseer.

Francis Chantree, Adam Kilgarriff, Anne De Roeck, and Alistair Willis. 2005. Disambiguating coordinations using word distribution information. *Proceedings of RANLP2005*.

Eugene Charniak and Mark Johnson. 2005. Coarse-to-fine n-best parsing and maxent discriminative reranking. In *Proceedings of the 43rd Annual Meeting of the Association for Computational Linguistics (ACL'05)*, pages 173–180, Ann Arbor, Michigan, June. Association for Computational Linguistics.

Andrew Clegg and Adrian Shepherd. 2007. Benchmarking natural-language parsers for biological applications using dependency graphs. *BMC Bioinformatics*, 8(1):24.

Kevin B. Cohen, Karin Verspoor, Helen L. Johnson, Chris Roeder, Philip V. Ogren, William A. Baumgartner Jr, Elizabeth White, Hannah Tipney, and Lawrence Hunter. 2009. High-precision biological event extraction with a concept recognizer. In *Proceedings of the Workshop on BioNLP: Shared Task*, pages 50–58. Association for Computational Linguistics.

Michael Collins. 2003. Head-driven statistical models for natural language parsing. *Computational linguistics*, 29(4):589–637.

Kazuo Hara, Masashi Shimbo, Hideharu Okuma, and Yuji Matsumoto. 2009. Coordinate structure analysis with global structural constraints and alignment-based local features. In *ACL-IJCNLP '09: Proceedings of the Joint Conference of the 47th Annual Meeting of the ACL and the 4th International Joint Conference on Natural Language Processing of the AFNLP: Volume 2*, pages 967–975, Morristown, NJ, USA. Association for Computational Linguistics.

Deirdre Hogan. 2007. Coordinate noun phrase disambiguation in a generative parsing model. In *Proceedings of the 45th Annual Meeting of the Association of Computational Linguistics*, pages 680–687, Prague, Czech Republic, June. Association for Computational Linguistics.

Thorsten Joachims. 1999. Making large scale SVM learning practical.

Mitchell P. Marcus, Beatrice Santorini, and Mary Ann Marcinkiewicz. 1994. Building a large annotated corpus of English: The Penn Treebank. *Computational linguistics*, 19(2):313–330.

Preslav Nakov and Marti Hearst. 2005. Using the web as an implicit training set: Application to structural ambiguity resolution. In *Proceedings of Human Language Technology Conference and Conference on Empirical Methods in Natural Language Processing*, pages 835–842, Vancouver, British Columbia, Canada, October. Association for Computational Linguistics.

Jens Nilsson, Joakim Nivre, and Johan Hall. 2006. Graph transformations in data-driven dependency parsing. In *Proceedings of the 21st International Conference on Computational Linguistics and 44th Annual Meeting of the Association for Computational Linguistics*, pages 257–264, Sydney, Australia, July. Association for Computational Linguistics.

Joakim Nivre and Ryan McDonald. 2008. Integrating graph-based and transition-based dependency parsers. In *Proceedings of ACL-08: HLT*, pages 950–958, Columbus, Ohio, June. Association for Computational Linguistics.

Philip Resnik. 1999. Semantic similarity in a Taxonomy: An Information-Based Measure and its Application to Problems of Ambiguity in Natural Language. *Journal of Artificial Intelligence*, 11(11):95–130.

Masashi Shimbo and Kazuo Hara. 2007. A discriminative learning model for coordinate conjunctions. In *Proceedings of the 2007 Joint Conference on Empirical Methods in Natural Language Processing and Computational Natural Language Learning (EMNLP-CoNLL)*, pages 610–619.

Andreas Stolcke. 2002. SRILM-an extensible language modeling toolkit. In *Seventh International Conference on Spoken Language Processing*, volume 3. Citeseer.

Yuka Tateisi, Akane Yakushiji, Tomoko Ohta, and Junichi Tsujii. 2005. Syntax Annotation for the GENIA corpus. In *Second International Joint Conference on Natural Language Processing (IJCNLP05)*, pages 222–227.

David Vadas and James Curran. 2007. Adding noun phrase structure to the penn treebank. In *Proceedings of the 45th Annual Meeting of the Association of Computational Linguistics*, pages 240–247, Prague, Czech Republic, June. Association for Computational Linguistics.

On Automated Evaluation of Readability of Summaries: Capturing Grammaticality, Focus, Structure and Coherence

Ravikiran Vadlapudi
Language Technologies Research Center
IIIT Hyderabad
ravikiranv@research.iiit.ac.in

Rahul Katragadda
Language Technologies Research Center
IIIT Hyderabad
rahul_k@research.iiit.ac.in

Abstract

Readability of a summary is usually graded manually on five aspects of readability: *grammaticality*, *coherence and structure*, *focus*, *referential clarity* and *non-redundancy*. In the context of automated metrics for evaluation of summary quality, content evaluations have been presented through the last decade and continue to evolve, however a careful examination of readability aspects of summary quality has not been as exhaustive. In this paper we explore alternative evaluation metrics for '*grammaticality*' and '*coherence and structure*' that are able to strongly correlate with manual ratings. Our results establish that our methods are able to perform pair-wise ranking of summaries based on grammaticality, as strongly as ROUGE is able to distinguish for content evaluations. We observed that none of the five aspects of readability are independent of each other, and hence by addressing the individual criterion of evaluation we aim to achieve automated appreciation of readability of summaries.

1 Introduction

Automated text summarization deals with both the problem of identifying relevant snippets of information and presenting it in a pertinent format. Automated evaluation is crucial to automatic text summarization to be used both to rank multiple participant systems in shared tasks[1], and to developers whose goal is to improve the summarization systems. Summarization evaluations help in the creation of reusable resources and infrastructure; it sets up the stage for comparison and replication of results by introducing an element of competition to produce better results (Hirschman and Mani, 2001).

Readability or Fluency of a summary is categorically measured based on a set of linguistic quality questions that manual assessors answer for each summary. The linguistic quality markers are: *grammaticality*, *Non-Redundancy*, *Referential Clarity*, *Focus* and *Structure and Coherence*. Hence *readability assessment* is a manual method where expert assessors give a rating for each summary on the Likert Scale for each of the linguistic quality markers. Manual evaluation being time-consuming and expensive doesn't help system developers — who appreciate fast, reliable and most importantly *automated* evaluation metric. So despite having a sound manual evaluation methodology for readability, there is an need for reliable automatic metrics.

All the early approaches like Flesch Reading Ease (Flesch, 1948) were developed for general texts and none of these techniques have tried to characterize themselves as approximations to grammaticality or structure or coherence. In assessing readability of summaries, there hasn't been much of dedicated analysis with text summaries, except in (Barzilay and Lapata, 2005) where local coherence was modeled for text summaries and in (Vadlapudi and Katragadda, 2010) where grammaticality of text summaries were explored. In a marginally related work in Natural Language Generation, (Mutton et al., 2007) addresses sentence level fluency regardless of content, while recent work in (Chae and Nenkova, 2009) gives a systematic study on how syntactic features were able to distinguish machine generated translations from human translations. In another related work, (Pitler and Nenkova, 2008) investigated the impact of certain *surface linguistic features*, *syntactic*, *entity coherence* and *discourse* features on the readability of Wall Street Journal (WSJ) Corpus. We use the *syntactic* features used in (Pitler and Nenkova, 2008) as baselines for our experiments on grammaticality in this paper.

[1] The summarization tracks at Text Analysis Conference (TAC) 2009, 2008 and its predecessors at Document Understanding Conferences (DUC).

Proceedings of the NAACL HLT 2010 Student Research Workshop, pages 7–12,
Los Angeles, California, June 2010. ©2010 Association for Computational Linguistics

While studying the coherence patterns in student essays, (Higgins et al., 2004) identified that grammatical errors affect the overall expressive quality of the essays. In this paper, due to the lack of an appropriate baseline and due to the interesting-ness of the above observation we use metrics for grammaticality as a baseline measure for *structure and coherence*. Focus of a summary, is the only aspect of readability that relies to a larger extent on the content of the summary. In this paper, we use Recall Oriented Understudy of Gisting Evaluation (ROUGE) (Lin, 2004) based metrics as one of the baselines to capture *focus* in a summary.

2 Summary Grammaticality

Grammaticality of summaries, in this paper, is defined based on the grammaticality of its sentences, since it is more a sentence level syntactic property. A sentence can either be grammatically correct or grammatically incorrect. The problem of grammatical incorrectness should not occur in summaries being evaluated because they are generated mostly by extract based summarization systems.

But as the distribution of grammaticality scores in Table 1 shows, there are a lot of summaries that obtain very low scores. Hence, We model the problem of grammaticality as "*how suitable or acceptable are the sentence structures to be a part of a summary?*".

The acceptance or non acceptance of sentence structures varies across reviewers because of various factors like usage, style and dialects. Hence, we define a degree to which a sentence structure is acceptable to the reviewers, this is called the *degree of acceptance* throughout this paper.

Grammaticality Score	1	2	3	4	5
Percentage Distribution (in %)	10	13	15	37	25

Table 1: Percentage distribution of grammaticality scores in system summaries

In this paper, the *degree of acceptance* of sentence structures is estimated using language models trained on a corpus of human written summaries. Considering the sentence structures in reference summaries as the best accepted ones (with highest *degree of acceptance*), we estimate the *degree of acceptance* of sentences in system generated summaries by quantifying the amount of similarity/digression from the references using the language models.

The structure of the sentences can be represented by sequences of parts-of-speech (POS) tags and chunk tags. Our previous observations (Vadlapudi and Katragadda, 2010) show that the tagset size plays an important role in determining the *degree of acceptance*. In this paper, we combine the two features of a sentence — the POS-tag sequence and chunk-tag sequence — to generate the POS-Chunk-tag training corpus.

Some aspects of grammatical structure are well identifiable at the level of POS tags, while some other aspects (such as distinguishing between appositives and lists for eg.) need the power of chunk tags, the combination of these two tag-sequences provides the power of both.

Hence, the following approaches use probabilistic models, learned on POS tag corpus and POS-Chunk tag corpus, in 3 different ways to determine the grammaticality of a sentence.

2.1 Enhanced Ngram model

As described in our previous work, the Ngram model estimates the probability of a sentence to be grammatically acceptable with respect to the corpus using language models. Sentences constructed using frequent grammar rules would have higher probability and are said to have a well accepted sentence structure. The grammaticality of a summary is computed as

$$G(Sum) = AVG(P(Seq_i)) \ ; \ P(Seq_i) = \log(\sqrt[n]{\prod_{j=1}^{n} P(K_j)})$$

$$P(K_j) = P(t_{j-2}t_{j-1}t_j)$$

$$P(t_1t_2t_3) = \lambda_1 * P(t_3|t_1t_2) + \lambda_2 * P(t_3|t_2) + \lambda_3 * P(t_3)$$

where $G(Sum)$ is grammaticality score of a summary Sum and $G(S_i)$ is grammaticality of sentence S_i which is estimated by the probability $(P(Seq_i))$ of its POS-tag sequence (Seq_i). $P(K_j)$ is probability of POS-tag trigram K_j which is $t_{j-2}t_{j-1}t_j$ and $\forall t_j, \ t_j \in POS \ tags$. The additional tags t_{-1}, t_0 and t_{n+1} are the beginning-of-sequence and end-of-sequence markers. The average AVG of the grammaticality scores of sentences $P(Seq_i)$ in a summary gives the final grammaticality score of the summary. In the prior work, arithmetic mean was used as the averaging technique, which performs consistently well. However, here two other averaging techniques namely *geometric mean* and *harmonic mean* are experimented and based on our experiments, we found *geometric mean* performing better than the other two averaging techniques. All the results reported in this paper are based on *geometric mean*. The above procedure estimates grammaticality of sentence using its POS tags and we call this run '*Ngram (POS)*'. A similar procedure is followed to estimate grammaticality using its POS-Chunk tags (language models trained on POS-chunk-tag training corpus). The corresponding run is called '*Ngram (POS-Chunk)*' in the results.

2.2 Multi-Level Class model

In this model, we view the task of scoring grammaticality as a n-level classification problem. Grammaticality of summaries is manually scored on a scale of 1 to 5, which means the summaries are classified into 5 classes. We assume that each sentence of the summary is also rated on a similar scale which cumulatively decides to which class the summary must belong. In our approach, sentences are classified into 5 classes on the basis of frequencies of underlying grammar rules (trigram) by defining class boundaries on frequencies. Hence, the cumulative score of the rules estimate the score of grammaticality of a sentence and inturn the summary.

Similar to (Vadlapudi and Katragadda, 2010), trigrams are classified into 5 classes C_1, C_2, C_3, C_4 and C_5 and each class is assigned a score on a similar scale ($\forall_j score(C_j) = j$) and class boundaries are estimated using the frequencies of trigrams in the training corpus. The most frequent trigram, for example, would fall into class C_5. POS-Class sequences are generated from POS-tag sequences using class boundaries as shown in Figure 1. This is the first level of classification.

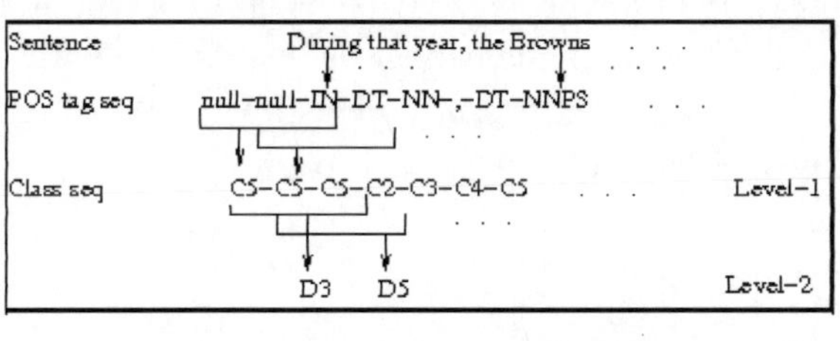

Figure 1: Two-level class model

Like the first level of classification, a series of classifications are performed upto 'k' levels. At each level we apply the scoring method described below to evaluate the grammaticality of summaries. We observed that from 3rd level onwards the structural dissimilarity disappears and the ability to distinguish different structures is lost. Hence, we report on the second level of classification, that captures the grammatical acceptability of summaries very well, and Figure 1 explains the two level classification.

$$G(S_i) = AVG(H(C_{w1}), H(C_{w2}), ..., H(C_{wn})) \quad (1)$$

AVG is the average of $H(C_{wi})$, where $w1$, $w2$, $\ldots wn$ are class trigrams, C_{wi} is the class into which class trigram wi falls into and $H(C_{wi})$ is score assigned to the class C_{wi}. The AVG is computed using geometric mean and this run is referred as '*Class (POS 2 level)*' in the results.

Similar to above approach, the grammaticality of a sentence can also be estimated using POS-Chunk tag sequence and POS-Chunk Class training data, and the corresponding run is referred as '*Class (POS-Chunk 2 level)*'.

2.3 Hybrid Model

As would be later seen in Table 2, the *Ngram (POS)* and *Class (POS 2 level)* runs are able to distinguish various systems based on grammaticality. We also note that these runs are able to very finely distinguish the degree of grammaticality at summary level. This is a very positive result, one that shows the applicability of applying these methods to any test summaries in this genre. To fully utilize these methods we combine the two methods by a linear combination of their scores to form a '*hybrid model*'. As seen with earlier approaches, both the POS-tag sequences and POS-Chunk-tag sequences could be used to estimate the grammaticality of a sentence, and hence the summary. These two runs are called '*Hybrid (POS)*' and '*Hybrid (POS-Chunk)*', respectively.

3 Structure and Coherence

Most automated systems generate summaries from multiple documents by extracting relevant sentences and concatenating them. For these summaries to be comprehensible they must also be *cohesive* and *coherent*, apart from being *content bearing* and *grammatical*. Lexical cohesion is a type of cohesion that arises from links between words in a text (Halliday and Hasan, 1976).A Lexical chain is a sequence of such related words spanning a unit of text. Lexical cohesion along with presuppositions and implications with world knowledge achieves coherence in texts. Hence, *coherence* is what makes text semantically meaningful, and in this paper, we also attempt to automate the evaluation of the "*structure and coherence*" of summaries.

We capture the structure or lexical cohesion of a summary by constructing a lexical chain that spans the summary. The relation between entities (noun phrases) in adjacent sentences could be of type center-reference (pronoun reference or reiteration), or based on semantic relatedness (Morris and Hirst, 1991). A center-reference relation exists if an entity in a sentence is a reference to center in adjacent sentence. Identifying centers of reference expressions can be done using a co-reference resolution tool. Performance of co-reference resolution tools in summaries, being evaluated, is not as good as their performance on generic texts. Semantic relatedness relation cannot be captured by using tools like Wordnet because they are not very exhaustive and hence are not effective. We use a much richer knowledge base to define this relation – Wikipedia.

Coherence of a summary is modelled by its structure and content together. Structure is captured by lexical chains which also give information about focus of each sentence which inturn contribute to the topic focus of the summary. Content presented in the summary must be semantically relevant to the topic focus of the summary. If the content presented by each sentence is semantically relevant to the focus of the sentence, then it would be semantically relevant to the topic focus of the summary. As the foci of sentences are closely related, a prerequisite for being a part of a lexical chain, the summary is said to be coherent. In this paper, the semantic relatedness of topic focus and content is captured using Wikipedia as elaborated in Section 3.1 of this paper.

3.1 Construction of lexical chains

In this approach, we identify the strongest lexical chain possible which would capture the structure of the summary. We define this problem of finding the strongest possible lexical chain as that of finding the best possible parts-of-speech tag sequence for a sentence using the Viterbi algorithm shown in (Brants, 2000). The entities (noun phrases) of each sentence are the nodes and transition probabilities are defined as relatedness score (Figure 2). The strongest lexical chain would have the highest score than other possible lexical chains obtained.

Consider sentence S_k with entity set (e_{11}, e_{12}, $e_{13}, \ldots e_{1n}$) and sentence S_{k+1} with entity set (e_{21}, e_{22}, e_{23}, $\ldots e_{2m}$). Sentences S_k and S_{k+1} are said to be strongly connected if there exists entities $e_{1i} \in S_k$ and $e_{2j} \in S_{k+1}$ that are closely related. e_{1i} and e_2j are considered closely related if

- e_{2j} is a pronoun reference of the center e_{1i}
- e_{2j} is a reiteration of e_{1i}
- e_{2j} and e_{1i} are semantically related

Pronoun reference In this approach, we resolve the reference automatically by finding more than one possible center for the reference expression using Wikipedia. Since the summaries are generated from news articles, we make a fair assumption that related articles are present in Wikipedia. We ensure that the correct center is one among the possible centers through which S_{k+1} and S_{k+2} might be strongly connected. Entities with *query hits ratio* $\geq \lambda$ are considered as possible centers and entity e_{2j} is replaced by entities that act as the possible centers. Since the chain with the identified correct center is likely to have the highest score, our final lexical chain would contain the correct center.

$$Query\ hit\ ratio = \frac{Query\ hits(e_{1i}\ and\ e_{2j})}{Query\ hits(e_{1i})}$$

Reiteration Generally, an entity with a determiner can be treated as reiteration expression but not vice versa. Therefore, we check whether e_{2j} is actually a reiteration expression or not, using query hits on Wikipedia. If *Query hits* $(e_{2j}) \geq\ \beta$ then we consider it to be a reiteration expression. A reiterating expression of a *named entity* is generally a common noun that occurs in many documents. After identifying a reiteration expression we estimate relatedness using semantic relatedness approach.

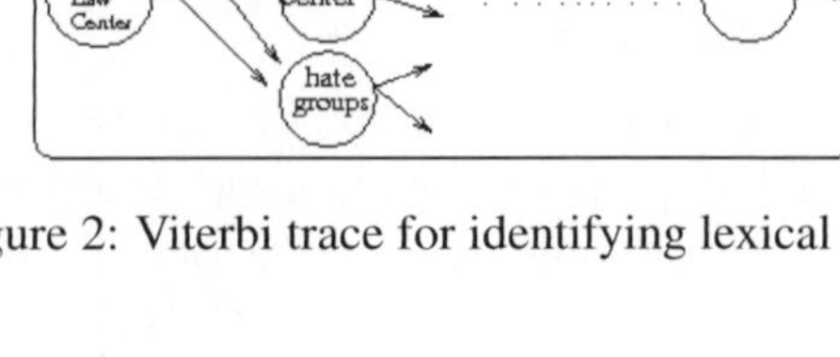

Figure 2: Viterbi trace for identifying lexical chain

Semantic relatedness By using *query hits* over Wikipedia we estimate the *semantic relatedness* of two entities. Such an approach has been previously attempted in (Strube and Ponzetto, 2006). Based on our experiments on grammaticality 2.2, classifying into 5 classes is better suited for evaluation tasks, hence we follow suit and classify *semantic relatedness* into 5 classes. These classes indicate how semantically related the entities are. Each class is assigned a value that is given to the hits which fall into the class. For example, if *query hits* lie in the range (γ_1, γ_2) or if query hit ratio is $\geq \xi$ then it falls into class k and is assigned a score equal to k.

Now that we have computed semantic connectedness between adjacent sentences using the methods explained above, we identify the output node with maximum score (node V2 in Figure 2). This node with best score is selected and by backtacking the Viterbi path we generate the lexical chain for the summary. The constants $\lambda, \gamma_1, \gamma_2and\xi$ are determined based on empirical tuning.

3.2 Coherence

We estimate coherence of the summary by estimating how the sentences stick together and the semantic relevance of their collocation. In a sentence, the semantic relatedness of entities with the focus estimates score for the meaningfulness of the sentence, and the average score of all the sentences estimates the coherence of the summary.

$$C(Summary) = \frac{\Sigma_{i=1}^{N} G(s_i)}{N}$$

$$G(s_i) = \frac{\Sigma_{j=1}^{k-1} H(Q(F \; and \; e_{ij}))}{k}$$

Where $C(Summary)$ is the coherence of summary $Summary$, and $G(s_i)$ is the semantic relatedness of a sentence s_i in $Summary$, while $Q(q)$ denotes the number of query hits of query q. F is the focus of s_i and e_{ij} is an entity in s_i, and $H(Q)$ is the score of class into which query falls.

4 Evaluation

This paper deals with methods that imitate manual evaluation metric for *grammaticality* and *structure and coherence* by producing a score for each summary. An evaluation of these new *summarization evaluation metrics* is based on how well the system rankings produced by them correlate with manual evaluations. We use 3 types of correlation evaluations — Spearman's Rank Correlation, Pearson's Correlation and Kendall's Tau — each describing some aspect of ordering problems.

We used reference summaries from TAC 2008, 2009 for the reference corpus and the experiments described were tested on DUC 2007 query-focused multi-document summarization datasets which have 45 topics and 32 system summaries for each topic apart from 4 human reference summaries.

Table 2 shows the system level correlations of our approaches to *grammaticality* assessment with that of human ratings. We have used four baseline approaches: AverageNPs, AverageVPs, AverageSBARs and AverageParseTreeHeight. Our approaches constitute of the following runs: *Ngram (POS), Ngram (POS-Chunk), Class (POS 2 level), Class (POS-Chunk 2 level), Hybrid (POS), Hybrid (POS-Chunk).*

RUN	Spearman's ρ	Pearson's r	Kendall's τ
	Baselines		
AverageNPs	0.1971	0.2378	0.1577
AverageSBARs	0.2923	0.4167	0.2138
AverageVPs	0.3118	0.3267	0.2225
ParseTreeHeight	0.2483	0.3759	0.1922
	Our experiments		
Ngram (POS)	0.7366	0.7411	0.5464
Ngram (POS+Chunk)	0.7247	0.6903	0.5421
Class (POS 2 level)	0.7168	0.7592	0.5464
Class (POS+Chunk 2 level)	0.7061	0.7409	0.5290
Hybrid (POS)	0.7273	**0.7845**	0.5205
Hybrid (POS+Chunk)	**0.7733**	0.7485	**0.5810**

Table 2: System level correlations of automated and manual metrics for grammaticality

RUN	Spearman's ρ	Pearson's r	Kendall's τ
	Experiments		
Ngram (POS)	**0.4319**	**0.4171**	**0.3165**
Ngram (POS+Chunk)	**0.4132**	**0.4086**	**0.3124**
Class (POS 2 level)	0.3022	0.3036	0.2275
Class (POS+Chunk 2 level)	0.2698	0.2650	0.2015
Hybrid (POS)	**0.3652**	**0.3483**	**0.2747**
Hybrid (POS+Chunk)	0.3351	0.3083	0.2498

Table 3: Summary level correlations of automated and manual metrics for *grammaticality* .

RUN	Spearman's ρ	Pearson's r	Kendall's τ
	Baselines		
Human Grammaticality rating	0.5546	**0.6034**	0.4152
Ngram(POS)	0.3236	0.4765	0.2229
	Experiments		
Our coherence model	**0.7133**	0.5379	**0.5173**

Table 4: System level correlations of automated and manual metrics for *coherence* .

Table 4 shows the system level correlations of our approach to *structure and coherence* assessment with that of human ratings. As mentioned earlier in Section 1, human ratings for grammaticality and our

RUN	Spearman's ρ	Pearson's r	Kendall's τ
	Baselines		
Human Grammaticality rating	0.5979	0.6463	0.4360
Human Coherence rating	0.9400	0.9108	0.8196
Ngram(POS)	0.4336	0.6578	0.3175
Our coherence model	0.5900	0.5331	0.4125
ROUGE-2	0.3574	0.4237	0.2681

Table 5: System level correlations of automated and manual metrics for *focus*

best performing system for grammaticality are used as baselines for *structure and coherence* assessment. Again, like we previously mentioned, *focus* can be easily characterized using structure and coherence, and to an extent the grammatical well-formedness. Also the *focus* of a summary is also dependent on content of the summary. Hence, we use ROUGE-2, manual rating for grammaticality, manual rating for coherence, and our approaches to both *grammaticality* and *structure and coherence* as baselines as shown in Table 5.

5 Discussion and Conclusion

In this paper, we addressed the problem of identifying the *degree of acceptance* of grammatical formations at sentence level using surface features like Ngrams probabilities (in Section 2.1), and trigrams based class Ngrams (in Section 2.2) and a hybrid model using both Ngram and Class model (in Section 2.3), on the POS-tag sequences and POS-chunk-tag sequences which have produced impressive results improving upon our previous work.

Our approaches have produced high correlations to human judgment on grammaticality. Results in Table 2 show that the Hybrid approach on the POS-Chunk tag sequences outperforms all the other approaches. Our approaches to grammaticality assessment have performed decently at pair-wise ranking of summaries, shown by correlations of the order of 0.4 for many runs. This correlation is of the same order as that of similar figure for content evaluations using ROUGE and Basic Elements.

Table 4 shows that our approach to the 'structure and coherence' assessment outperforms the baselines set and has an impressive correlation with manual ratings. From Table 5 we found that grammaticality is a good indicator of focus while we also observe that *structure and coherence* forms a strong alternative to *focus*.

The focus of this paper was on providing a complete picture on capturing the grammaticality aspects of readability of a summary using relatively shallow features as POS-tags and POS-Chunk-tags. We used lexical chains to capture *structure and coherence* of summaries, whose performance also correlated with *focus* of summaries. None of the five aspects of readability are completely independent of each other, and by addressing the individual criteria for evaluation we aim to achieve overall appreciation of readability of summary.

References

Regina Barzilay and Mirella Lapata. 2005. Modeling local coherence: An entity-based approach. In *ACL*.

Thorsten Brants. 2000. Tnt: a statistical part-of-speech tagger. In *Proceedings of the sixth conference on Applied natural language processing*, pages 224–231, Morristown, NJ, USA. Association for Computational Linguistics.

Jieun Chae and Ani Nenkova. 2009. Predicting the fluency of text with shallow structural features: Case studies of machine translation and human-written text. In *EACL*, pages 139–147. The Association for Computer Linguistics.

Rudolf Flesch. 1948. A new readability yardstick. *Journal of Applied Psychology*, 32:221–233.

M.A.K Halliday and Ruqayia Hasan. 1976. Longman publishers.

Derrick Higgins, Jill Burstein, Daniel Marcu, and Claudia Gentile. 2004. Evaluating multiple aspects of coherence in student essays. In *HLT-NAACL 2004: Main Proceedings*, pages 185–192, Boston, Massachusetts, USA, May 2 - May 7. Association for Computational Linguistics.

Lynette Hirschman and Inderjeet Mani. 2001. Evaluation.

Chin-Yew Lin. 2004. ROUGE: A Package for Automatic Evaluation of Summaries. In *the proceedings of ACL Workshop on Text Summarization Branches Out*. ACL.

Jane Morris and Graeme Hirst. 1991. Lexical cohesion computed by thesaural relations as an indicator of the structure of text. *Comput. Linguist.*, 17(1):21–48.

Andrew Mutton, Mark Dras, Stephen Wan, and Robert Dale. 2007. Gleu: Automatic evaluation of sentence-level fluency. In *ACL*. The Association for Computer Linguistics.

Emily Pitler and Ani Nenkova. 2008. Revisiting readability: A unified framework for predicting text quality. In *EMNLP*, pages 186–195. ACL.

Michael Strube and Simone Paolo Ponzetto. 2006. Wikirelate! computing semantic relatedness using wikipedia. In *21. AAAI / 18. IAAI 2006*. AAAI Press, july.

Ravikiran Vadlapudi and Rahul Katragadda. 2010. Quantitative evaluation of grammaticality of summaries. In *CICLing*.

Detecting Novelty in the context of Progressive Summarization

Praveen Bysani
Language Technologies Research Center
IIIT Hyderabad
lvsnpraveen@research.iiit.ac.in

Abstract

A Progressive summary helps a user to monitor changes in evolving news topics over a period of time. Detecting novel information is the essential part of progressive summarization that differentiates it from normal multi document summarization. In this work, we explore the possibility of detecting novelty at various stages of summarization. New scoring features, Re-ranking criterions and filtering strategies are proposed to identify "relevant novel" information. We compare these techniques using an automated evaluation framework ROUGE, and determine the best. Overall, our summarizer is able to perform on par with existing prime methods in progressive summarization.

1 Introduction

Summarization is the process of condensing text to its most essential facts. Summarization is challenging for its associated cognitive task and interesting because of its practical usage. It has been successfully applied for text content such as news articles [1], scientific papers (Teufel and Moens, 2002) that follow a discourse structure. Update summarization is an emerging area with in summarization, acquiring significant research focus during recent times. The task was introduced at DUC 2007[2] and continued during TAC 2008, 2009[3]. We refer to update summariztion as "Progressive Summarization" in rest of this paper, as summaries are produced periodically in a progressive manner and the latter title is more apt to the task. Progressive summaries contain information which is both relevant and novel, since they are produced under the assumption that user has already read some previous documents/articles on the topic. Such summaries are extremely useful in tracking news stories, tracing new product reviews etc.

Unlike dynamic summarization (Jatowt, 2004) where a single summary transforms periodically, reflecting changes in source text, Progressive summarizer produce multiple summaries at specific time intervals updating user knowledge. Temporal Summarization (Allan et al., 2001) generate summaries, similar to progressive summaries by ranking sentences as combination of *relevant and new* scores. In this work, summaries are produced not just by reforming ranking scheme but also altering scoring and extraction stages of summarization.

Progressive summarization requires differentiating *Relevant and Novel* Vs *Non-Relevant and Novel* Vs *Relevant and Redundant* information. Such discrimination is feasible only with efficient Novelty detection techniques. We define Novelty detection as identifying relevant sentences containing new information. This task shares similarity with TREC Novelty Track [4], that is designed to investigate systems abilities to locate sentences containing relevant and/or new information given the topic and a set of relevant documents ordered by date. A progressive summarizer needs to identify, score and then finally rank "relevant novel" sentences to produce a summary.

[1] http://newsblaster.cs.columbia.edu/
[2] http://duc.nist.gov/duc2007/tasks.html
[3] http://www.nist.gov/tac
[4] http://trec.nist.gov/data/novelty.html

Proceedings of the NAACL HLT 2010 Student Research Workshop, pages 13–18,
Los Angeles, California, June 2010.

Previous approaches to Novelty detection at TREC (Soboroff, 2004) include cosine filtering (Abdul-Jaleel et al., 2004), where a sentence having maximum cosine similarity value with previous set of sentences, lower than a preset threshold is considered novel. Alternatively, (Schiffman and McKeown, 2004) considered previously unseen words as an evidence of Novelty. (Eichmannac et al., 2004) expanded all noun phrases in a sentence using wordnet and used corresponding sysnsets for novelty comparisions.

Our work targets exploring the effect of detecting novelty at different stages of summarization on the quality of progressive summaries. Unlike most of the previous work (Li et al., 2009) (Zhang et al., 2009) in progressive summarization, we employ multiple novelty detection techniques at different stages and analyze them all to find the best.

2 Document Summarization

The Focus of this paper is only on extractive summarization, henceforth term summarization/summarizer implies sentence extractive multi document summarization. Our Summarizer has 4 major stages as shown in Figure 1,

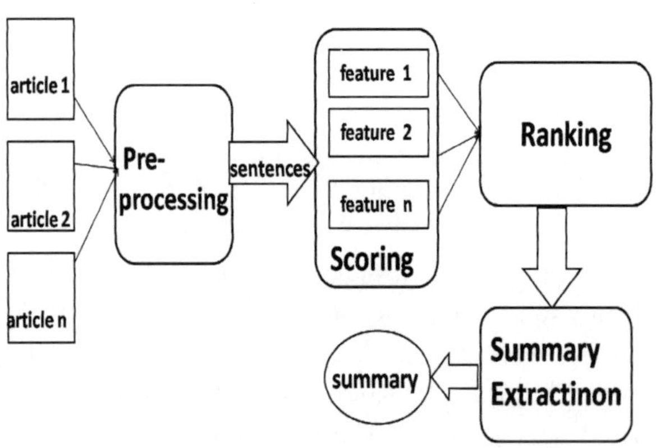

Figure 1: Stages in a Multi Document Summarizer

Every news article/document is cleaned from news heads, HTML tags and split into sentences during *Pre-processing* stage. At *scoring*, several sentence scoring features assign scores for each sentence, reflecting its topic relevance. Feature scores are combined to get a final rank for the sentence in *ranking* stage. Rank of a sentence is predicted from regression model built on feature vectors of sentences in the training data using support vector machine as explained in (Schilder and Kondadandi, 2008). Finally during *summary extraction*, a subset of ranked sentences are selected to produce summary after a redundancy check to filter duplicate sentences.

2.1 Normal Summarizers

Two normal summarizers (*DocSumm, TacBaseline*) are developed in a similar fashion described in Figure 1.

DocSumm produce summaries with two scoring features, Document Frequency Score (DF) (Schilder and Kondadandi, 2008) and Sentence Position (SP). DocSumm serves as a baseline to depict the effect of novelty detection techniques described in Section 3 on normal summarizers. *Document frequency (DF)*, of a word (w) in the document set ($docs$) is defined as ratio of number of documents in which it occured to the total number of documents. Normalized DF score of all content words in a sentence is considered its feature score.

$$DF_{docs}(w) = \frac{\{|d| : w \in d\}}{|docs|}$$

Sentence Position (SP) assigns positional index (n) of a sentence (s_n) in the document (d) it occurs as its feature score. Training model will learn the optimum sentence position for the dataset.

$$SP(s_{nd}) = n$$

TacBaseline is a conventional baseline at TAC, that creates a n word length summary from first n words of the most recent article. It provides a lower bound on what can be achieved with automatic multi document summarizers.

3 Novelty Detection

Progressive summaries are generated at regular time intervals to update user knowledge on a particular news topic. Imagine a set of articles published on a evolving news topic over time period T, with t_d being publishing timestamp of article d. All the articles published from time 0 to time t are assumed to have been read previously, hence prior knowledge, $pdocs$. Articles published in the interval t to T that contain new information are considered $ndocs$.

$$ndocs = \{d : t_d > t\}$$
$$pdocs = \{d : t_d <= t\}$$

Progressive summarization needs a novelty detection technique to identify sentences that contain relevant new information. The task of detecting novelty can be carried out at 3 stages of summarization shown in Figure 1.

3.1 At Scoring

New Sentence scoring features are devised to capture sentence novelty along with its relevance. Two features Novelty Factor (NF) (Varma et al., 2009), and New Words (NW) are used at scoring level.

Novelty Factor (NF)

NF measures both topic relevancy of a sentence and its novelty given prior knowledge of the user through $pdocs$. NF score for a word w is calculated as,

$$NF(w) = \frac{|nd_t|}{|pd_t| + |ndocs|}$$

$nd_t = \{d : w \in d \wedge d \in ndocs\}$
$pd_t = \{d : w \in d \wedge d \in pdocs\}$
$|nd_t|$ captures the relevancy of w, and $|pd_t|$ elevates the novelty by penalizing words occurring frequently in $pdocs$. Score of a sentence is the average NF value of its content words.

New Words (NW)

Unlike NF, NW captures only novelty of a sentence. Novelty of a sentence is assessed by the amount of *new* words it contains. Words that never occurred before in $pdocs$ are considered *new*. Normalized term frequency of a word (w) is used in calculating feature score of sentence. Score of a sentence(s) is given by,

$$\begin{aligned} Score(s) &= \frac{\sum_{w \in s} NW(w)}{|s|} \\ NW(w) &= 0 \quad if \ w \in pdocs \\ &= n/N \quad else \end{aligned}$$

n is frequency of w in $ndocs$
N is total term frequency of $ndocs$

3.2 At Ranking

Ranked sentence set is re-ordered using Maximal Marginal relevance (Carbonell and Goldstein, 1998) criterion, such that prior knowledge is neglected and sentences with new information are promoted in the ranked list. Final rank ("Rank") of a sentence is computed as,

$$\begin{aligned} Rank &= relweight * rank - \\ &\quad (1 - relweight) * redundancy\_score \end{aligned}$$

Where "rank" is the original sentence rank predicted by regression model as described in section 2, and "redundancy_score" is an estimate for the amount of prior information a sentence contains. Parameter "relweight" adjusts relevancy and novelty of a sentence. Two similarity measures *ITSim, CoSim* are used for calculating redundancy_score.

Information Theoretic Similarity (ITSim)

According to information theory, Entropy quantifies the amount of information carried with a message. Extending this analogy to text content, Entropy $I(w)$ of a word w is calculated as,

$$I(w) = -p(w) * log(p(w))$$
$$p(w) = n/N$$

Motivated by the information theoretic definition of similarity by (Lin, 1998), we define similarity between two sentences $s1$ and $s2$ as,

$$ITSim(s1, s2) = \frac{2 * \sum_{w \in s1 \wedge s2} I(w)}{\sum_{w \in s1} I(w) + \sum_{w \in s2} I(w)}$$

Numerator is proportional to the commonality between $s1$ and $s2$ and denominator reflects differences between them.

Cosine Similarity (CoSim)

Cosine similarity is a popular technique in TREC Novelty track to compute sentence similarity. Sentences are viewed as tf-idf vectors (Salton and Buckley, 1987) of words they contain in a *n-dimension* space. Similarity between two sentences is measured as,

$$CoSim(s1, s2) = cos(\Theta) = \frac{s1.s2}{|s1||s2|}$$

Average similarity value of a sentence with all sentences in $pdocs$ is considered as its redundancy score.

3.3 At summary extraction

Novelty Pool (NP)

Sentences that possibly contain prior information are filtered out from summary by creating Novelty Pool (NP), a pool of sentences containing one or more $novelwords$. Two sets of "dominant" words are generated one for each $pdocs$ and $ndocs$.

$$dom_{ndocs} = \{w : DF_{ndocs}(w) > threshold\}$$

$$dom_{pdocs} = \{w : DF_{pdocs}(w) > threshold\}$$

A word is considered dominant if it appears in more than a predefined "threshold " of articles, thus measuring its topic relevance. Difference of the two dom sets gives us a list of $novelwords$ that are both relevant and new.

$$novelwords = dom_{ndocs} - dom_{pdocs}$$

4 Experiments and Results

We conducted all the experiments on TAC 2009 Update Summarization dataset. It consists of 48 topics, each having 20 documents divided into two clusters "A" and "B" based on their chronological coverage of topic. It serves as an ideal setting for evaluating our progressive summaries. Summary for cluster A (*pdocs*) is a normal multi document summary where as summary for cluster B (*ndocs*) is a Progressive summary, both of length 100 words. Each topic has associated 4 model summaries written by human assessors. TAC 2008 Update summarization data that follow similar structure is used to build training model for support vectors as mentioned in Section 2. Thresholds for dom_{ndocs}, dom_{pdocs} are set to 0.6, 0.3 respectively and *relweight* to 0.8 for optimal results.

Summaries are evaluated using ROUGE (Lin, 2004), a recall oriented metric that automatically assess machine generated summaries based on their overlap with models. ROUGE-2 and ROUGE-SU4 are standard measures for automated summary evaluation. In Table 1 ROUGE scores of baseline systems(Section 2.1) are presented.

Five progressive runs are generated, each having a novelty detection scheme at either scoring, ranking or summary extraction stages. ROUGE scores of these runs are presented in Table 2.

	ROUGE-2	**ROUGE-SU4**
DocSumm	0.09346	0.13233
TacBaseline	0.05865	0.09333

Table 1: Average ROUGE-2, ROUGE-SU4 recall scores of $baselines$ for TAC 2009, cluster B

NF+DocSumm : Sentence scoring is done with an additional feature NF, along with default features of DocSumm

NW+DocSumm : An additional feature NW is used to score sentences for DocSumm

ITSim+DocSumm : ITSim is used for computing similarity between a sentence in *ndocs* and set of all sentences in *pdocs*. Maximum similarity value is considered as redundancy_score. Re-ordered ranked list is used for summary extraction

Cosim+DocSumm : CoSim is used as a similarity measure instead of ITSim

NP+DocSumm : Only members of NP are considered while extracting DocSumm summaries

Results of top systems at TAC 2009, *ICSI* (Gillick et al., 2009) and *THUSUM* (Long et al., 2009) are also provided for comparison.

	ROUGE-2	**ROUGE-SU4**
ICSI	0.10417	0.13959
NF+DocSumm	0.10273	0.13922
NW+DocSumm	0.09645	0.13955
NP+DocSumm	0.09873	0.13977
THUSUM	0.09608	0.13499
ITSim+DocSumm	0.09461	0.13306
Cosim+DocSumm	0.08338	0.12607

Table 2: Average ROUGE-2, ROUGE-SU4 recall scores for TAC 2009, cluster B

Next level of experiments are carried out on combination of these techniques. Each run is produced by combining two or more of the above(Section 3) described techniques in conjunction with $DocSumm$. Results of these runs are presented in table 3

NF+NW : Both NF and NW are used for sentence scoring along with default features of DocSumm

NF+NW+ITSim : Sentences scored in NF+NW are re-ranked by their ITSim score

NF+NW+NP : Only members of NP are selected while extracting NF+NW summaries

NF+NW+ITSim+NP : Sentences are selected from NP during extraction of NF+NW+ITSim summaries

	ROUGE-2	ROUGE-SU4
NF+NW	0.09807	0.14058
NF+NW+ITSim	0.09704	0.13978
NF+NW+NP	0.09875	0.14010
{NP+NW+ ITSim+NP}	0.09664	0.13812

Table 3: Average ROUGE-2, ROUGE-SU4 recall scores for TAC 2009, cluster B

5 Conclusion and Discussion

Experimental results prove that proposed Novelty Detection techniques, particularly at scoring stage are very effective in the context of progressive summarization. Both NF, a language modeling technique and NW, a heuristic based feature are able to capture relevant novelty successfully. An approximate 6% increase in ROUGE-2 and 3% increase in ROUGE-SU4 scores over DocSumm support our argument. Scores of NF+DocSumm and NW+DocSumm are comparable with existing best approaches. Since CoSim is a word overlap measure, and novel information is often embedded within a sentence containing formerly known information, quality of progressive summaries declined. ITSim performs better than Cosim because it considers entropy of a word in similarity computations, which is a better estimate of information. There is a need for improved similarity measures that can capture semantic relatedness between sentences. Novelty pool (NP) is a simple filtering technique, that improved quality of progressive summaries by discarding probable redundant sentences into summary. From the results in Table 2, it can be hypothesized that Novelty is best captured at sentence scoring stage of summarization, rather than at ranking or summary extraction.

A slight improvement of ROUGE scores is observed in table 3, when novelty detection techniques at scoring, ranking and extracting stages are combined together. As Novel sentences are already scored high through NF and NW, the effect of Re-Ranking and Filtering is not significant in the combination.

The major contribution of this work is to identify the possibility of novelty detection at different stages of summarization. Two new sentence scoring features (NF and NW), a filtering strategy (NP), a sentence similarity measure (ITSim) are introduced to capture relevant novelty. Although proposed approaches are simple, we hope that this novel treatment could inspire new methodologies in progressive summarization. Nevertheless, the problem of progressive summarization is far from being solved given the complexity involved in novelty detection.

Acknowledgements

I would like to thank Dr. Vasudeva Varma at IIIT Hyderabad, for his support and guidance throughout this work. I also thank Rahul Katragadda at Yahoo Research and other anonymous reviewers, for their valuable suggestions and comments.

References

Nasreen Abdul-Jaleel, James Allan, W. Bruce Croft, Fernando Diaz, Leah Larkey, and Xiaoyan Li. 2004. Umass at trec 2004: Novelty and hard.

James Allan, Rahul Gupta, and Vikas Khandelwal. 2001. Temporal summaries of news topics.

Jaime Carbonell and Jade Goldstein. 1998. The use of mmr, diversity-based reranking for reordering documents and producing summaries. In *SIGIR '98: Proceedings of the 21st annual international ACM SIGIR conference on Research and development in information retrieval*, pages 335–336, New York, NY, USA. ACM.

David Eichmannac, Yi Zhangb, Shannon Bradshawbc, Xin Ying Qiub, Padmini Srinivasanabc, and Aditya Kumar. 2004. Novelty, question answering and genomics: The university of iowa response.

Dan Gillick, Benoit Favre, Dilek Hakkani-Tur, Berndt Bohnet, Yang Liu, and Shasha Xie. 2009. The icsi/utd summarization system at tac 2009.

Adam Jatowt. 2004. Web page summarization using dynamic content. In *WWW Alt. '04: Proceedings of the 13th international World Wide Web conference on Alternate track papers and posters*, pages 344–345, New York, NY, USA. ACM.

Sujian Li, Wei Wang, and Yongwei Zhang. 2009. Tac 2009 update summarization with unsupervised methods.

Dekang Lin. 1998. An information-theoretic definition of similarity. In *ICML '98: Proceedings of the Fifteenth International Conference on Machine Learn-*

ing, pages 296–304, San Francisco, CA, USA. Morgan Kaufmann Publishers Inc.

Chin-Yew Lin. 2004. Rouge: A package for automatic evaluation of summaries. pages 74–81, Barcelona, Spain, July. Association for Computational Linguistics.

Chong Long, Minlie Huang, and Xiaoyan Zhu. 2009. Tsinghua university at tac 2009: Summarizing multi-documents by information distance.

Gerard Salton and Chris Buckley. 1987. Term weighting approaches in automatic text retrieval. Technical report, Ithaca, NY, USA.

Barry Schiffman and Kathleen R. McKeown. 2004. Columbia university in the novelty track at trec 2004.

Frank Schilder and Ravikumar Kondadandi. 2008. Fastsum: fast and accurate query-based multi-document summarization. In *Proceedings of the 46th Annual Meeting of the Association for Computational Linguistics on Human Language Technologies*. Human Language Technology Conference.

Ian Soboroff. 2004. Overview of the trec 2004 novelty track. National Institute of Standards and Technology,Gaithersburg, MD 20899.

Simone Teufel and Marc Moens. 2002. Summarizing scientific articles: experiments with relevance and rhetorical status. *Comput. Linguist.*, 28(4):409–445.

Vasudeva Varma, Praveen Bysani, Kranthi Reddy, Vijay Bharat, Santosh GSK, Karuna Kumar, Sudheer Kovelamudi, Kiran Kumar N, and Nitin Maganti. 2009. iiit hyderabad at tac 2009. Technical report, Gaithersburg, Maryland USA.

Jin Zhang, Pan Du, Hongbo Xu, and Xueqi Cheng. 2009. Ictgrasper at tac2009: Temporal preferred update summarization.

Extrinsic Parse Selection

David Goss-Grubbs
University of Washington
Department of Linguistics
Box 354340
Seattle, WA 98195-4340, USA
davidgg@u.washington.edu

Abstract

This paper reports on one aspect of Locutus, a natural language interface to databases (NLIDB) which uses the output of a high-precision broad-coverage grammar to build semantic representations and ultimately SQL queries. Rather than selecting just a subset of the parses provided by the grammar to use in further processing, Locutus uses all of them. If the meaning of a parse does not conform to the semantic domain of the database, no query is built for it. Thus, intended parses are chosen extrinsically. The parser gives an average of 3.01 parses to the sentences in the GEOQUERY250 corpus. Locutus generates an average of 1.02 queries per sentence for this corpus, all of them correct.

1 Introduction

Natural language sentences are typically more ambiguous than the people who utter them or perceive them are aware of. People are very good at using context and world knowledge to unconsciously disambiguate them. High-precision, broad-coverage grammars, however, often assign every legitimate analysis to a given sentence, even when only one of them reflects the sentence's intended meaning. It is thus important for natural language processing applications that use these analyses to be able to reliably select the intended parse. It is typical for such applications to choose the best parse up front and pass just that one on to further processing. For some applications, however, it is possible, and indeed preferable, to pass all the parses on and let downstream processing decide which parses to use.

This paper describes such an application. Locutus (Goss-Grubbs to appear), a natural language interface to relational databases (NLIDB), creates semantic representations for the parses assigned by a high-precision broad-coverage grammar, and from those creates SQL queries. It does not include a step where one or more "best" parses are selected for further processing. Queries are built for all parses for which it is possible to do so. For a standard corpus of NLIDB training sentences, it is able to generate the correct query whenever a suitable analysis is given by the parser. In the rare case where it generates two queries, both queries are equally correct.

2 Parse Selection

Parse selection for probabilistic grammars involves simply finding the most probable parse, or top-N most probable parses, and can be done using efficient algorithms, (e.g. Klein and Manning, 2003).

Things are different for high-precision, hand-coded grammars, such as the LinGO English Resource Grammar, ERG (Flickinger, 2000), a Head-Driven Phrase Structure Grammar implementation of English; and Xerox's English grammar (Butt, et al., 2002), a Lexical Functional Grammar implementation. These grammars do not define a probability distribution over parses. Rather, they assign to each string all of its grammatically valid

Proceedings of the NAACL HLT 2010 Student Research Workshop, pages 19–22,
Los Angeles, California, June 2010.

parses. Techniques for deciding between parses produced by these kinds of grammars include using sortal constraints on arguments of semantic relations (Müller and Kasper, 2000); and annotating individual grammatical rules with weights (Kiefer, et al., 1999). More recently, the development of rich treebanks such as the LinGO Redwoods (Oepen, et al., 2004) which stores all analyses of a sentence, along with an indication of which is the preferred one, makes it possible to train maximum entropy models for parse selection, (e.g. Toutanova, et al., 2002).

For at least the NLIDB task, however, selection of the best parse is not an end in itself. Rather, what is necessary is to generate the intended database query. Indeed, two or more distinct syntactic parses may all lead to the same (intended) query. If the NLIDB identifies this query correctly, it has achieved its goal without, strictly speaking, having selected the best parse.

Furthermore, eliminating any grammatically valid parse without subjecting it to further processing risks missing the intended query. For these reasons, Locutus does no intrinsic parse selection. Rather, it tries to build a query for all valid parses. The semantic constraints of the database domain limit well-formed semantic representations to those that make sense in that domain, so that a grammatically valid parse may not receive a legitimate semantic representation, and thus not receive a database query.

3 Locutus

Locutus is an NLIDB which is designed to be portable with respect to source language and grammatical formalism. It can take as input the syntactic analyses produced by any sufficiently sophisticated grammar/parser. The implementation reported on in this paper consumes the f-structures produced by the Xerox English grammar.

Locutus is also portable with respect to database domain. The projection of semantic structures from the syntactic analyses provided by the parser is guided by a semantic description of the database domain together with a set of constraints called *sign templates* linking syntactic patterns with semantic patterns.

High precision (building only correct queries) is maintained in a number of ways:

- High-precision syntactic grammars are used.
- The projection of semantic structures from syntactic structures is resource-sensitive. Every element of the syntactic structure must be referenced just once by the sign template that licenses the corresponding semantic structure.
- The semantic description of the database domain defines a network of semantic relationships and their arguments, along with constraints regarding which arguments are compatible with one another. In this way, semantic structures which would otherwise be generated can be ruled out.

3.1 Processing Pipeline

The processing of a sentence by Locutus proceeds in the following way. The string of words is passed to the XLE parser, which returns a contextualized feature structure from which individual parses are extracted. An example parse appears in Figure 1.

```
[ PRED border
  SUBJ [ PRED state
         NTYPE [ NSYN common ]
         SPEC [ DET [ PRED which
                      NTYPE [ NSYN … ]
                      PRON-TYPE int ] ]
         CASE nom
         NUM pl
         PERS 3 ]
  OBJ [ PRED delaware
        NTYPE [ NSYN proper ]
        CASE obl
        NUM sg
        PERS 3 ]
  PRON-INT [...]
  FOCUS-INT [...]
  TNS-ASP [...]
  CLAUSE-TYPE int
  PASSIVE -
  VTYPE main ]
```

Figure 1: parse for “Which states border delaware?”

Locutus interprets this syntactic analysis into a set of semantic representations called Semantic Mobile Structures, an example of which appears in an abbreviated form in Figure 2.

```
x0 DefQuant: [ > [1]]
   r0 Border:STATE1
        STATE2: x1 DefQuant: [1]
                   r1 StateName:STATE
                        NAME: [delaware]
   r2 State:STATE
```

Figure 2: SMS for "Which states border delaware?"

Finally, this representation is translated into an SQL query, as shown in Figure 3, which is sent to the database, and the answer is shown.

```
select t1.Name
from border, state t1, state t2
where border.State1 = t1.Name and
      border.State2 = t2.Name and
      t2.Name = 'delaware'
```

Figure 3: query for "Which states border Delaware?"

3.2 Efficiency

There is a bit of time savings in not having an intrinsic parse-selection step. These savings are counterbalanced by the extra time it takes to interpret parses that would have otherwise been excluded by such a step. However, a certain amount of syntactic structure is shared among the various parses of a syntactically ambiguous sentence. Locutus recognizes when a piece of syntactic structure has already been interpreted, and reuses that interpretation in every parse in which it appears. In this way Locutus minimizes the extra time taken to process multiple parses. At any rate, processing speed does not appear to be a problem at this point in the development of Locutus.

3.3 Further Work

Although Locutus has a wide range of functionality, it is still a work in progress. The format for authoring sign templates is rather complex, and customizing Locutus for a given database can be time-consuming. I anticipate an authoring tool which makes much of the customization process automatic, and hides much of the complexity of the rest of the process from the author, but such a tool has yet to be implemented.

4 Experiment

To test the coverage and precision of Locutus, I have customized it to answer questions from the GEOQUERY 250 corpus (Mooney, 1996), which consists of a database of geographical information paired with 250 English sentences requesting information from that database. 25 of these sentences are held out for the purposes of another study, and I have not examined the behavior of Locutus with respect to these sentences. I ran the other 225 sentences through Locutus, keeping track of which sentences Locutus built at least one query for. For each of those sentences, I also tracked the following:

- How many syntactic parses were generated by the grammar
- How many queries were produced
- How many of those queries were correct

The XLE Engine includes a facility to do stochastic disambiguation (Kaplan, et al. 2004), and the English grammar I used comes with a property weights file of the kind required by the disambiguation process. I ran the sentences through Locutus using just the single best parse returned by that process, keeping track of how many queries were produced.

5 Results

223 of the 225 sentences (99.1%) are assigned at least one query. For the other two sentences, no analysis returned by the parser reflect the intended meaning of the sentence. The average number of parses for these sentences is 3.01, with 158 sentences given at least two parses, and 84 sentences given at least three. Some sentences were given as many as 20 parses.

Figure 4 contains the graph of the number of parses by the average number of queries assigned to sentences with that many parses. Note that the number of queries per sentence is not correlated with the number of parses assigned by the grammar. The sentences that were assigned more than one query were each assigned either one or two parses. All the sentences with more syntactic parses were assigned a single query each.

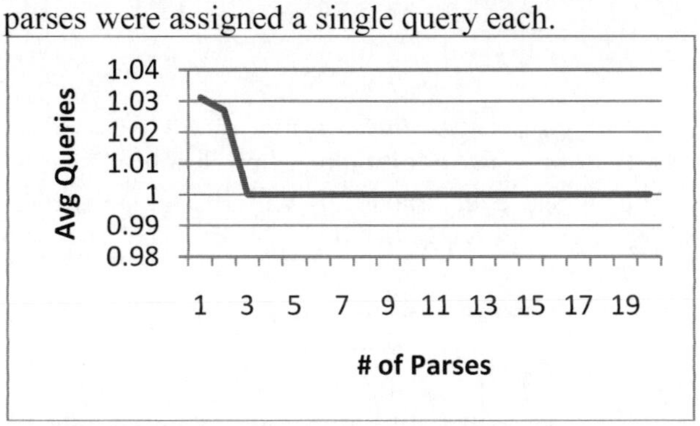

Figure 4: Average queries by ambiguity level

Of the 223 sentences that were assigned a query, 219 of them were assigned exactly one query. Every query was correct in the sense that it accurately reflected a reasonable interpretation of the sentence. Four sentences were each assigned two queries. They are given in (1)-(4).

(1) How many people live in Washington?
(2) How many people live in New York?
(3) What is the length of the Colorado river?
(4) What is the length of the Mississippi river?

It is appropriate that each of these sentences gets two queries. For (1)-(2), the GEOQUERY 250 database contains cities, their populations, states and their populations; "Washington" and "New York" are both names of cities and states that appear in the database. For (3)-(4), one interpretation is to return the length of the river mentioned in the sentence. The other possibility is to return all the rivers that are the same lengths as the ones mentioned. For instance, in the GEOQUERY database, the Colorado and Arkansas rivers are both 2333 km long. One valid answer to (3) is the number "2333". The other valid answer is the list of rivers "Arkansas" and "Colorado". To give any of these sentences only a single query would be to miss a reasonable interpretation.

Table 1 summarizes the results when only a single parse for each sentence, chosen stochastically using the property weights file provided with the XLE English grammar, is sent to Locutus. The parse is considered correct if it leads to a correct query.

	# of sents	avg. parses	% correct
≥ 1 parse	223	3.01	54%
≥ 2 parses	158	3.84	35%

Table 1

Although performance is better than chance, it is clearly less successful than when Locutus is allowed to use every parse, in which case a correct query is always constructed.

6 Conclusion

For natural language processing applications that take the results of a high-precision syntactic parser and pass them along to further processing, selecting the correct parse is not an end in itself. It is only useful insofar as it improves the final result.

For applications such as NLIDBs, which are provided with a precise semantic framework within which sentences may be interpreted, it is better to pass along the full set of grammatically valid parses than to select beforehand a limited subset of those parses. Using this technique, Locutus achieves 100% correctness on the sentences for which it builds a query.

References

Butt, Miriam, Helge Dyvik, Tracy Holloway King, Hiroshi Masuichi, and Christian Rohrer. "The Parallel Grammar Project." *Proceedings of COLING2002 Workshop on Grammar Engineering and Evaluation.* 2002.

Flickinger, Dan. "On building a more efficient grammar by exploiting types." *Natural Language Engineering* 6, no. 1 (2000): 15-28.

Goss-Grubbs, David. "Deep Processing for a Portable Natural Language Interface to Databases." *dissertation, University of Washington.* to appear.

Kaplan, Ron, Stefan Riezler, Trace King, John Maxwell, Alexander Vasserman, and Richard Crouch. "Speed and Accuracy in Shallow and Deep Stochastic Parsing." *Proceedings of the Human Language Technology Conference and the 4th Annual Meeting of the North American Chapter of the Association for Computational Linguistics (HLT-NAACL'04).* Boston, MA, 2004.

Kiefer, Bernd, Hans-Ulrich Krieger, John Carroll, and Rob Malouf. "A Bag of Useful Techniques for Efficient and Robust Parsing." *Proceedings of the 37th Meeting of the Association for Computational Linguistics.* College Park, MD, 1999. 473-480.

Klein, Dan, and Christopher D. Manning. "A* Parsing: Fast Exact Viterbi Parse Selection." *Proceedings of HLT-NAACL 2003.* 2003. 40-47.

Mooney, Raymond. *Geoquery Data.* 1996. http://www.cs.utexas.edu/users/ml/nldata/geoquery.html (accessed February 13, 2010).

Müller, Stefan, and Walter Kasper. "HPSG Analysis of German." In *Verbmobil. Foundations of Speech-to-Speech Translation*, edited by Wolfgang Wahlster, 238-253. Berlin: Springer, 2000.

Oepen, Stephan, Dan Flickinger, Kristina Toutanova, and Christopher D. Manning. "LinGO Redwoods: A Rich and Dynamic Treebank for HPSG." *Research on Language and Computation* (Springer) 2 (2004): 575-596.

Toutanova, Kristina, Christopher D. Manning, Stuart Shieber, Dan Flickinger, and Stephan Oepen. "Parse disambiguation for a rich HPSG grammar." *Proceedings of the First Workshop on Treebanks and Linguistic Theories.* 2002. 253-263.

Towards a Matrix-based Distributional Model of Meaning

Eugenie Giesbrecht
FZI Forschungszentrum Informatik
at the University of Karlsruhe
Haid-und-Neu-Str. 10-14, Karlsruhe, Germany
giesbrecht@fzi.de

Abstract

Vector-based distributional models of semantics have proven useful and adequate in a variety of natural language processing tasks. However, most of them lack at least one key requirement in order to serve as an adequate representation of natural language, namely sensitivity to structural information such as word order. We propose a novel approach that offers a potential of integrating order-dependent word contexts in a completely unsupervised manner by assigning to words characteristic distributional matrices. The proposed model is applied to the task of free associations. In the end, the first results as well as directions for future work are discussed.

1 Introduction

In natural language processing as well as in information retrieval, Vector Space Model (VSM) (Salton et al., 1975) and Word Space Model (WSM) (Schütze, 1993; Lund and Burgess, 1996) have become the mainstream for text representation. VSMs embody the distributional hypothesis of meaning, the main assumption of which is that a word is known "by the company it keeps" (Firth, 1957). VSMs proved to perform well in a number of cognitive tasks such as synonymy identification (Landauer and Dumais, 1997), automatic thesaurus construction (Grefenstette, 1994) and many others. However, it has been long recognized that these models are too weak to represent natural language to a satisfactory extent. With VSMs, the assumption is made that word co-occurrence is essentially independent of word order. All the co-occurrence information is thus fed into one vector per word.

Suppose our "background knowledge" corpus consists of one sentence: *Peter kicked the ball.* It follows that the distributional meanings of both PETER and BALL would be in a similar way defined by the co-occurring KICK which is insufficient, as BALL can be only *kicked* by somebody but not *kick* itself; in case of PETER, both ways of interpretation should be possible. To overcome the aforementioned problems with vector-based models, we suggest a novel distributional paradigm for representing text in that we introduce a further dimension into a "standard" two-dimensional word space model. That allows us to count correlations for three words at a time. In short, given a vocabulary V, context width $w = m$ and tokens $t_1, t_2, t_3, ..., t_i \in V$, for token t_i a matrix of size $V \times V$ is generated that has nonzero values in cells where t_i appears between t_{i-m} and t_{i+m}.

Note that this 3-dimensional representation allows us to integrate word order information into the model in a completely unsupervised manner as well as to achieve a richer word representation as a matrix instead of a vector.

The remainder of the paper is organized as follows. After a recap of basic mathematical notions and operations used in the model in Section 2, we introduce the proposed three-dimensional tensor-based model of text representation in Section 3. First evaluation experiments are reported in Section 4.

Proceedings of the NAACL HLT 2010 Student Research Workshop, pages 23–28,
Los Angeles, California, June 2010.

After a brief overview of related work in Section 5, we provide some concluding remarks and suggestions for future work in Section 6.

2 Preliminaries

In this section, we provide a brief introduction to tensors and the basics of mathematical operations that are employed in the suggested model.

First, given d natural numbers $n_1, \ldots, n_d$, a *(real)* $n_1 \times \ldots \times n_d$ *tensor* can be defined as a function $T : \{1, \ldots, n_1\} \times \ldots \times \{1, \ldots, n_d\} \rightarrow \mathbb{R}$, mapping d-tuples of natural numbers to real numbers. Intuitively, a tensor can best be thought of as a d-dimensional table (or array) carrying real numbers as entries. Thereby $n_1, \ldots, n_d$ determine the extension of the array in the different directions. Obviously, matrices can be conceived as $n_1 \times n_2$-tensors and vectors as n_1-tensors.

In our setting, we will work with tensors where $d = 3$ and for the sake of better understandability we will introduce the necessary notions for this case only.

Our work employs *higher-order singular value decomposition* (HOSVD), which generalizes the method of singular value decomposition (SVD) from matrices to arbitrary tensors.

Given an $n_1 \times n_2 \times n_3$ tensor T, its *Tucker decomposition* (Tucker, 1966) for given natural numbers m_1, m_2, m_3 consists of an $m_1 \times m_2 \times m_3$ tensor G and three matrices A, B, and C of formats $n_1 \times m_1$, $n_2 \times m_2$, and $n_3 \times m_3$, respectively, such that

$$T(i,j,k) = \sum_{r=1}^{m_1} \sum_{s=1}^{m_2} \sum_{t=1}^{m_3} G(r,s,t) \cdot A(i,r) \cdot B(j,s) \cdot C(k,t).$$

The idea here is to represent the large-size tensor T by the smaller "core" tensor G. The matrices A, B, and C can be seen as linear transformations "compressing" input vectors from dimension n_i into dimension m_i. Note that a precise representation of T is not always possible. Rather one may attempt to approximate T as well as possible, i.e. find the tensor T' for which a Tucker decomposition exists and which has the least distance to T. Thereby, the notion of distance is captured by $\|T - T'\|$, where $T - T'$ is the tensor obtained by entry-wise subtraction and $\| \cdot \|$ is the *Frobenius norm* defined by

$$\|M\| = \sqrt{\sum_{r=1}^{n_1} \sum_{s=1}^{n_2} \sum_{t=1}^{n_3} (M(r,s,t))^2}.$$

In fact, the described way of approximating a tensor is called *dimensionality reduction* and is often used for reducing noise in multi-dimensional data.

3 Proposed Model

Our motivation is to integrate structure into the geometrical representation of text meaning while adhering to the ideas of distributional semantics. For this, we introduce a third dimension that allows us to separate the left and right contexts of the words. As we process text, we accumulate the left and right word co-occurrences to represent the meaning of the current word. Formally, given a corpus $\mathcal{K}$, a list L of tokens, and a context width w, we define its tensor representation $T_{\mathcal{K}}$ by letting $T_{\mathcal{K}}(i,j,k)$ be the number of occurrences of $L(j)\ s\ L(i)\ s'\ L(k)$ in sentences in $\mathcal{K}$ where s, s' are (possibly empty) sequences of at most $w - 1$ tokens. For example, suppose our corpus consists of three sentences: "Paul kicked the ball slowly. Peter kicked the ball slowly. Paul kicked Peter." We let $w = 1$, presuming prior stop words removal. We obtain a $5 \times 5 \times 5$ tensor. Table 1 displays two i-slices of the resulting tensor T showing left vs. right context dependencies.

KICK	PETER	PAUL	KICK	BALL	SLOWLY
PETER	0	0	0	1	0
PAUL	1	0	0	1	0
KICK	0	0	0	0	0
BALL	0	0	0	0	0
SLOWLY	0	0	0	0	0

BALL	PETER	PAUL	KICK	BALL	SLOWLY
PETER	0	0	0	0	0
PAUL	0	0	0	0	0
KICK	0	0	0	0	2
BALL	0	0	0	0	0
SLOWLY	0	0	0	0	0

Table 1: Slices of T for the terms KICK ($i = 3$) and BALL ($i = 4$).

Similarly to traditional vector-based distributional models, dimensionality reduction needs to be performed in three dimensions either, as the resulting tensor is very sparse (see the examples of KICK and

BALL). To this end, we employ Tucker decomposition for 3 dimensions as introduced in Section 2. For this, Matlab Tensor Toolbox[1] (Bader and Kolda, 2006) is used.

A detailed overview of computational complexity of Tucker decomposition algorithms in Tensor Toolbox is provided in Turney (2007). The drawback of those is that their complexity is cubic in the number of factorization dimensions and unfeasible for large datasets. However, new memory efficient tensor decomposition algorithms have been proposed in the meantime. Thus, *Memory Efficient Tucker (MET)* is available in Matlab Tensor Toolbox since Version 2.3. Rendle and Schmidt-Thieme (2010) present a new factorization method with linear complexity.

4 Evaluation Issues

4.1 Task

Vector-based distributional similarity methods have proven to be a valuable tool for a number of tasks on automatic discovery of *semantic relatedness* between words, like synonymy tests (Rapp, 2003) or detection of analogical similarity (Turney, 2006).

A somewhat related task is the task of finding out to what extent (statistical) similarity measures correlate with free word associations[2]. Furthermore, this task was suggested as a *shared task* for the evaluation of word space models at Lexical Semantics Workshop at ESSLLI 2008. *Free associations* are the words that come to the mind of a native speaker when he or she is presented with a so-called *stimulus word*. The percent of test subjects that produce certain *response* to a given *stimulus* determines the degree of a free association between a *stimulus* and a *response*.

Despite the widespread usage of vector-based models to retrieve semantically similar words, it is still rather unclear what type of linguistic phenomena they model (cf. Heylen et al. (2008), Wandmacher et al. (2008)). The same is true for *free associations*. There are a number of relations according to which a word may be associated with another word. For example, Aitchison (2003) distinguishes four types of associations: co-ordination, collocation, superordination and synonymy. This affords an opportunity to use the task of *free associations* as a "baseline" for distributional similarity.

For this task, workshop organizers have proposed three subtasks, one of which - *discrimination* - we adapt in this paper. Test sets have been provided by the workshop organizers. The former are based on the Edinburgh Associative Thesaurus[3] (EAT), a freely available database of English association norms.

Discrimination task includes a test set of overall 300 word pairs that were classified according to three classes of association strengths:

- FIRST strongly associated word pairs as indicated by more than 50% of test subjects as first responses;
- HAPAX word associations that were produced by a single test subject;
- RANDOM random combinations of words from EAT that were never produced as a *stimulus - response* pair.

4.2 Procedure

To collect the three-way co-occurrence information, we experiment with the UKWAC corpus (A. Ferraresi and Bernardini, 2008), as suggested by the workshop organizers, in order to get comparable results. As UKWAC is a huge Web-derived corpus consisting of about 2 billion tokens, it was impossible at the current stage to process the whole corpus. As the subsections of UKWAC contain randomly chosen documents, one can train the model on any of the subsections.

We limited out test set to the word pairs for which the constituent words occur more than 50 times in the test corpus. Thereby, we ended up with a test set consisting of 222 word pairs.

We proceed in the following way. For *each pair of words*:

1. Gather N sentences, i.e. contexts, for each of the two words[4], here $N = 50$;

[1] Version 2.3

[2] One of the reasons to choose this evaluation setting was that the dataset for *free word associations task* is freely available at http://wordspace.collocations.de/doku.php/data:esslli2008:start (in contrast to, e.g., the synonymy test set).

[3] http://www.eat.rl.ac.uk/

[4] This corpus "preprocessing" step was mainly due to lim-

2. Build a 3-dimensional tensor from the subcorpus obtained in (1), given a context width w=5, i.e. 5 words to the left and 5 words to the right of the target word), taking sentence boundaries into consideration;

3. Reduce 5 times the dimensionality of the tensor obtained in (2) by means of Tucker decomposition;

4. Extract two matrices of both constituents of the word pair and compare those by means of cosine similarity[5].

Here, we follow the tradition of vector-based models where *cosine* is usually used to measure *semantic relatedness*. One of the future direction in matrix-based meaning representation is to investigate further matrix comparison metrics.

4.3 Results and Discussion

Tables 2 and 3 show the resulting accuracies[6] for training and test sets. th denotes cosine threshold values that were used for grouping the results. Here, th is taken to be the function of the size s of the data set. Thus, given a training set of size $s = 60$ and 3 classes, we define an "equally distributed" threshold $th_1 = 60/3 = 20$ (s. Table 2) and a "linearly growing" threshold $th_2 = \frac{1}{4}, \frac{1}{3}, rest$ (s. Table 3).

It is not quite apparent, how the threshold for differentiating between the groups should be determined under given conditions. Usually, such measures are defined on the basis of training data (e.g. Wandmacher et al. (2008)). It was not applicable in our case as, due to the current implementation of the model as well as insufficient computational resources for the time being, we could not build one big model for all experiment iterations.

Also, the intuition we have gained with this kind of thresholds is that as soon as you change the underlying corpus or the model parameters, you may need to define new thresholds (cf. Tables 2 and 3). Thresholds in geometric models of meaning can not be just fixed, just as the measure of similarity cannot be easily quantified by humans.

It would be straightforward to compare the performance of the proposed model with its 2-dimensional analogue. Wandmacher et al. (2008) obtain in average better results with their LSA-based model for this task. Specifically, they observe very good results for RANDOM associations (78.2% accuracy) but the lowest results for the FIRST, i.e. strongest, associations (50%). In constrast, the outcome for RANDOM in our model is the worst. However, the bigger the threshold, the more accurate is getting the model for the FIRST associations. For example, with a threshold of $th = 0.2$ for the test set - 4 out of 5 highest ranked pairs were highly associated (FIRST) and the fifth pair was from the HAPAX group. For HAPAX word associations, no similar regularities could be observed.

The resulting accuracies may seem to be poor at this stage. However, it is worth mentioning that this is a highly difficult and corpus-dependent task for automatic processing. The reported results have been obtained based on very small corpora, containing ca. 100 sentences per iteration (cf. Wandmacher et al. (2008) use a corpus of 108 million words to train their LSA-Model). Consequently, it is not possible to compare both results directly, as they have been produced under very different conditions.

5 Related Work

5.1 Matrix Approaches

There have been a number of efforts to integrate syntax into vector-based models with alternating success. Some used (dependency) parsing to feed the models (Grefenstette, 1994; Lin, 1998; Padó and Lapata, 2007); the others utilized only part of speech information, e.g., Widdows (2003).

In many cases, these syntactically enhanced models improved the performance (Grefenstette, 1994; Lin, 1998; Padó and Lapata, 2007). Sometimes, however, rather controversial results were observed. Thus, Widdows (2003) reported both positive and negative effects for the task of developing taxonomies. On the one side, POS information increased the performance for common nouns; on the other side, it degraded the outcome for proper nouns

ited processing power we had at our disposal at the moment the experiments were conducted. With this step, we considerably reduced the size of the corpus and guaranteed a certain number of contexts per relevant word.

[5]Cosine similarity is determined as a normalized inner product

[6]Accuracy is defined in the following way: $Accuracy = right/(right + wrong)$

	TRAIN	TEST
FIRST	12/20 (60%) ($th = 0.022$)	25/74 (33%) ($th = 0.078$))
HAPAX	7/20 (35%) ($th = 0.008$)	35/74 (47%) $th = 0.042$)
RANDOM	8/20 (40%)	23/74 (31%)
TOTAL (F/H/R)	27/60 (45%)	83/222 (37.4%)
FIRST/HORR[7]	44/60 (73.33%)	125/222 (56.3%)

Table 2: Accuracies for the "equally distributed" threshold for training and test sets

	TRAIN	TEST
FIRST	9/15 (60%) ($th = 0.0309$)	20/55 (36.4%) ($th = 0.09$)
HAPAX	8/20 (40%) ($th = 0.0101$)	39/74 (52.7%) ($th = 0.047$)
RANDOM	10/25 (40%)	24/93 (25.8%)
TOTAL (F/H/R)	27/60 (45%)	108/222 (48.6%)
FIRST/HORR[8]	43/60 (71.60%)	113/222 (50.9%)

Table 3: Accuracies for a "linearly growing" threshold for training and test sets

and verbs.

Sahlgren et al. (2008) incorporate word order information into context vectors in an unsupervised manner by means of permutation.

Recently, Erk and Padó (2008) proposed a structured vector space model where a word is represented by several vectors reflecting the words lexical meaning as well as its selectional preferences. The motivation behind their work is very close to ours, namely, that single vectors are too weak to represent word meaning. However, we argue that a matrix-based representation allows us to integrate contextual information in a more general manner.

5.2 Tensor Approaches

Among the early attempts to apply higher-order tensors instead of vectors to text data is the work of Liu et al. (2005) who show that Tensor Space Model is consistently better than VSM for text classification. Cai et al. (2006) suggest a 3-dimensional representation for documents and evaluate the model on the task of document clustering.

The above as well as a couple of other projects in this area in information retrieval community leave open the question of h*ow to convey text into a three-dimensional tensor*. They still use vector-based representation as the basis and then just mathematically convert vectors into tensors, without linguistic justification of such transformations.

Further, there are few works that extend the term-document matrix with metadata as a third dimension (Chew et al., 2007; Sun et al., 2006).

Turney (2007) is one of the few to study the application of tensors to word space models. However, the emphasis in that paper is more on the evaluation of different tensor decomposition models for such spaces than on the formal model of text representation in three dimensions. Van de Cruys (2009) suggests a three-way model of co-occurrence similar to ours. In contrast to Van de Cruys (2009), we are not using any explicit syntactic preprocessing. Furthermore, our focus is more on the model itself as a general model of meaning.

6 Summary and Future Work

In this paper, we propose a novel approach to text representation inspired by the ideas of distributional semantics. In particular, our model suggests a solution to the problem of integrating word order information in vector spaces in an unsupervised manner. First experiments on the task of free associations are reported. However, we are not in the position yet to commit ourselves to any representative statements. A thorough evaluation of the model still needs to be done. Next steps include, amongst others, evaluating the suggested model with a bigger data corpus as well as using stemming and more sophisticated filling of word matrices, e.g., by introducing advanced weighting schemes into the matrices instead of simple counts.

Furthermore, we started with evaluation on the task which has been proposed for the evaluation of word space models at the level of word meaning. We need, however, to evaluate the model for the tasks where word order information matters more, e.g. on selectional preferences or paraphrasing.

Last but not least, we plan to address the issue of modeling compositional meaning with matrix-based distributional model of meaning.

Acknowledgments

This work is supported by German "Federal Ministry of Economics" (BMWi) under the project Theseus (number 01MQ07019). Many thanks to the anonymous reviewers for their insightful comments.

References

M. Baroni A. Ferraresi, E. Zanchetta and S. Bernardini. 2008. Introducing and evaluating ukWaC, a very large Web-derived corpus of English. In *Proceedings of the WAC4 Workshop at LREC'08*.

Jean Aitchison. 2003. *Words in the Mind: An Introduction to the Mental Lexicon*. Wiley-Blackwell.

Brett W. Bader and Tamara G. Kolda. 2006. Algorithm 862: Matlab tensor classes for fast algorithm prototyping. *ACM Trans. Math. Softw.*, 32(4):635–653.

Deng Cai, Xiaofei He, and Jiawei Han. 2006. Tensor space model for document analysis. In *SIGIR*, pages 625–626. ACM.

Peter Chew, Brett Bader, Tamara Kolda, and Ahmed Abdelali. 2007. Cross-language information retrieval using PARAFAC2. In *Proc. KDD'07*, pages 143–152. ACM.

Katrin Erk and Sebastian Padó. 2008. A structured vector space model for word meaning in context. In *EMNLP*, pages 897–906. ACL.

J.R. Firth. 1957. A synopsis of linguistic theory 1930-55. *Studies in linguistic analysis*, pages 1–32.

Gregory Grefenstette. 1994. *Explorations in Automatic Thesaurus Discovery*. Springer.

Kris Heylen, Yves Peirsman, Dirk Geeraerts, and Dirk Speelman. 2008. Modelling word similarity: an evaluation of automatic synonymy extraction algorithms. In *Proceedings of LREC'08*, pages 3243–3249.

T. K. Landauer and S. T Dumais. 1997. Solution to Plato's Problem: The Latent Semantic Analysis Theory of Acquisition, Induction and Representation of Knowledge. *Psychological Review*, 104(2):211–240.

Dekang Lin. 1998. Automatic retrieval and clustering of similar words. In *Proceedings of ACL'98*, pages 768–774. ACL.

Ning Liu, Benyu Zhang, Jun Yan, Zheng Chen, Wenyin Liu, Fengshan Bai, and Leefeng Chien. 2005. Text representation: from vector to tensor. In *Proc. ICDM05*.

Kevin Lund and Curt Burgess. 1996. Producing high-dimensional semantic spaces from lexical co-occurrence. *Behavior Research Methods, Instrumentation, and Computers*, pages 203–20.

Sebastian Padó and Mirella Lapata. 2007. Dependency-based construction of semantic space models. *Computational Linguistics*, 33(2):161–199.

Reinhard Rapp. 2003. Word sense discovery based on sense descriptor dissimilarity. In *Proceedings of the Ninth Machine Translation Summit*, pages 315–322.

Steffen Rendle and Lars Schmidt-Thieme. 2010. Pairwise interaction tensor factorization for personalized tag recommendation. In *WSDM '10: Proceedings of the third ACM international conference on Web search and data mining*, pages 81–90, New York, NY, USA. ACM.

M. Sahlgren, A. Holst, and P. Kanerva. 2008. Permutations as a means to encode order in word space. In *Proc. CogSci08*, pages 1300–1305.

G. Salton, A. Wong, and C. S. Yang. 1975. A vector space model for automatic indexing. *Commun. ACM*, 18(11):613–620.

Hinrich Schütze. 1993. Word space. In *Advances in NIPS 5*, pages 895–902.

J. Sun, D. Tao, and C. Faloutsos. 2006. Beyond streams and graphs: Dynamic tensor analysis. In *Proc. KDD'06*, pages 374–383.

L.R. Tucker. 1966. Some mathematical notes on three-mode factor analysis. *Psychometrika*, 31(3).

Peter D. Turney. 2006. Similarity of semantic relations. *Computational Linguistics*, 32(3):379–416.

P. Turney. 2007. Empirical evaluation of four tensor decomposition algorithms. Technical report. Technical Report ERB-1152.

Tim Van de Cruys. 2009. A non-negative tensor factorization model for selectional preference induction. In *GEMS '09: Proceedings of the Workshop on Geometrical Models of Natural Language Semantics*, pages 83–90, Morristown, NJ, USA. ACL.

Tonio Wandmacher, Ekaterina Ovchinnikova, and Theodore Alexandrov. 2008. Does Latent Semantic Analysis reflect human associations. In *Proceedings of the Lexical Semantics workshop at ESSLLI*, Hamburg, Germany.

Dominic Widdows. 2003. Unsupervised methods for developing taxonomies by combining syntactic and statistical information. In *Proceedings of NAACL'03*, pages 197–204. ACL.

Distinguishing Use and Mention in Natural Language

Shomir Wilson
Computer Science
University of Maryland
College Park, MD 20742, USA
shomir@umd.edu

Abstract

When humans communicate via natural language, they frequently make use of metalanguage to clarify what they mean and promote a felicitous exchange of ideas. One key aspect of metalanguage is the mention of words and phrases, as distinguished from their use. This paper presents ongoing work on identifying and categorizing instances of language-mention, with the goal of building a system capable of automatic recognition of the phenomenon. A definition of language-mention and a corpus of instances gathered from Wikipedia are discussed, and the future direction of the project is described.

1 Introduction

Costello: Well then who's on first?
Abbott: Yes.
Costello: I mean the fellow's name.
Abbott: Who.
Costello: The guy on first.
Abbott: Who.

In Abbott and Costello's famous routine "Who's on First?", Costello asks Abbott for the names of the players on a baseball team. In the above excerpt[1], Abbott tries unsuccessfully to explain that the name of the first baseman is *Who*, but Costello interprets this as another question instead of a response to his own. If Abbott had been more explicit and less terse (by responding with "The fellow's name is the word 'Who'", for instance), he would have avoided the ambiguity in his answers and might have succeeded in conveying to Costello the name of the first baseman. Instead, this misunderstanding is repeated throughout the routine with comic results, as the two become increasingly agitated by their breakdown in communication.

As Abbott and Costello unwittingly demonstrated, we sometimes must refer to the language that we speak and write in order to understand language itself. *Metalanguage* is our facility for doing this, and its interpretation often implicitly relies on the *use-mention distinction*—that is, simply, the distinction between using elements of language and mentioning them. In both written and spoken communication, the mention of letters, sounds, words, phrases, or entire sentences (termed *language-mention* in this paper for brevity) is essential for indicating titles, explaining meaning, introducing new words, attributing exact utterances to others, and other common functions of metalanguage (Saka 2005). There is evidence that human conversation makes frequent use of the use-mention distinction, and that we would be severely handicapped without it (Perlis et al., 1998). Moreover, this distinction has close ties to the appearance-reality distinction in cognitive science (Miller 1993).

It is surprising, then, that the use-mention distinction has thus far received little attention in computational linguistics. The need for greater study is unmistakable, as human audiences gener-

[1] Quoted from `http://www.phoenix5.org/humor/WhoOnFirst.html`.

Proceedings of the NAACL HLT 2010 Student Research Workshop, pages 29–33,
Los Angeles, California, June 2010.

ally navigate through this linguistic phenomenon with a natural ease that computers do not possess. The complexity behind this natural ease is apparent in our ability to understand simple sentences such as "Sky is spelled S K Y" and "The letters S, K, and Y make the word sky", which mean essentially the same thing but are structured and worded very differently. To gain the benefits of understanding the use-mention distinction, natural language processing systems must detect the subtle cues that signal this phenomenon.

This paper presents some preliminary results from a project on characterizing and identifying instances of language-mention in the English language. The use-mention distinction is first explained in greater detail, and a working definition is proposed for the phenomenon of language-mention. A corpus of instances of language-mention from Wikipedia is then introduced, with analysis of the categories in which the phenomenon appears to occur. The hypothesis of this continuing project is that lexical and syntactic cues will be sufficient to automatically identify at least a large subset of instances of mentioned language.

2 The Use-Mention Distinction

The use-mention distinction, as previously stated, is the distinction between using linguistic entities (such as letters, sounds, words, phrases, or entire sentences) and mentioning them. Since this explanation is slightly opaque at best and possibly circular, some examples and a proposal for a definition are appropriate. Consider the following sentences:

(1) The cat is on the mat.

(2) The word "cat" is spelled with three letters.

In (1), the reader's attention to meaning does not focus on the words themselves, but instead upon the presumed cat on the mat. In (2), the reader understands that the word *cat*—a string of three letters, as opposed to any particular cat or an abstract idea of a cat—is in the focus of the sentence. Quotation marks around *cat* in (2) are a convention to further reinforce that the word is being mentioned, and in some contexts (such as this sentence) italics may serve the same purpose.

The other linguistic entities listed above can also be mentioned, and the reader may easily conjure appropriate examples. Of particular note is *quotation*, a form of language-mention in which language from another source is reproduced as part of a statement, as in (3) below:

(3) Eric said, "We should meet for lunch."

In (3), the phrase between quote marks is mentioned as what Eric has said. However, the reader is likely to treat the quoted text in (3) as a string with semantic depth, indicating that the *use* half of the use-mention distinction is present as well. Examples such as this illustrate that use and mention are not mutually exclusive (Maier 2007).

If writers always and consistently used cues such as quotation marks and italics, and if speakers followed a convention for delimiting mentioned utterances[2], recognizing language-mention would be an easier task. However, it frequently falls upon the intuition of the audience to determine when, where, and how it occurs (Anderson et al. 2002). Sentences (2) and (3) above, if typed less formally (sans quotation marks) or transcribed from speech, would still be easily understood by a human reader. Moreover, cues such as italics and quotation marks are also used for other purposes, such as distancing ("scare quotes") and emphasis, meaning that they are uncertain indicators of language-mention. It seems that subtler cues are responsible for our ability to distinguish use and mention.

In spite of the ubiquity of the phrase *use-mention distinction*, it is difficult to find an explicit definition for either the distinction itself or its two halves. The effort here will be to define language-mention, since this will aid in identifying where and how it occurs. What follows is a working definition, in the sense that it is a "rough draft"; suggestions for improvement are invited. For the moment, it restricts the scope of this work to *sentential* language-mention, where the mentioned linguistic entity is referred to inside of the same sentence that it occurs. (An example of a sentence that fails this additional requirement is: "Disregard the last thing I said.") This restriction is necessary to reduce the complexity of the identification and labeling problems, and it will be assumed for the rest of the paper.

Definition: For T a token or a set of tokens in a sentence, if T refers to a property of the token T or the type of T, then T is an instance of language-mention.

---

[2] One might observe that spoken language sometimes contains nonverbal cues for language-mention. While worthy of study, these cues fall beyond the scope of this paper, which will focus on written or transcribed language.

Here, a *token* can be any one of the linguistic entities listed at the beginning of this section—letters, sounds, words, phrases, or entire sentences. A *property* might be its spelling, pronunciation, original source (in the case of quotation), meaning (for a variety of interpretations of that term), or another aspect for which language is shown or demonstrated[3]. The *type* of T is relevant in some instances of language-mention (such as in (2)) and the *token* itself is relevant in others (including unusual cases such as "*The* is the first word in this sentence").

3 A Language-Mention Corpus

The second task of this project has been to create a corpus of sentences that contain instances of language-mention. The corpus will be valuable to move beyond laboratory examples and to begin mining for patterns in syntax and vocabulary that predict the occurrence of the phenomenon.

Wikipedia was chosen as a source of text for several reasons. Its text is freely available and covers a wide variety of subjects. Articles are written to be informative, which suggests that new names and terms are introduced frequently—a common function of language-mention. Contributors tend to highlight language-mention with italicization, bold text, or quotation marks. (This convention is mentioned in the Wikipedia Manual of Style, though it is unclear whether most contributors read it there or simply follow it out of habit.) While language-mention can certainly occur outside of those stylistic cues, the decision was made to concentrate on sentences that contained them, since this greatly accelerated the annotation process.

The annotation effort focused on the markup text of 1000 randomly chosen articles from English Wikipedia. Except for delimiters for bold and italic text, most of the markup was removed, and the remaining text was segmented into sentences using NLTK's implementation of the Punkt sentence tokenizer (Kiss and Strunk, 2006). The sentences then were filtered for only those that contained bold text, italic text, or text between single or double quotation marks, yielding a set of 1339 sentences that contained one or more of them.

Hand annotation required approximately three person-hours, with that time heavily skewed toward approximately the first third of the sentences, as the set of categories for language-mention was also developed during this labeling process. Categories were formed with an informal "diagnostic test" of substitution of the category's theme (e.g., "this proper name", "this translation", "this symbol", "this quotation") in the place of the candidate token or tokens. Only text highlighted by one of the cues mentioned above was considered for labeling. Although only one researcher participated in the annotation, at the time of writing this paper an effort was in progress to build a much larger corpus using multiple annotators via Amazon's Mechanical Turk service. This service has shown promise in other natural language annotation tasks (Snow et al., 2008).

Out of the 1339 sentences inspected by hand, 171 contained at least one instance of language-mention. Many of those sentences contained several instances. Table 1 below lists the categories observed and the frequencies of each one, and Table 2 provides examples from each category.

Language-Mention Category	Frequency
Proper name (PN)	119
Translation or Transliteration (TR)	61
Attributed Language (AT)	47
Words/Phrases as Themselves (WD)	46
Symbols/Nonliteral Marks (SY)	8
Phonetic/Sound (PH)	2
Spelling (SP)	2
Abbreviation (AB)	1

Table 1: Frequencies of the different categories of language-mention found in the corpus.

Cat.	Example
PN	In 2005, Ashley Page created another short piece on Scottish Ballet, a strikingly modern piece called "The Pump Room", set to pulsating music by Aphex Twin.
TR	The Latin title translates as "a method for finding curved lines enjoying properties of maximum or minimum, or solution of isoperimetric problems in the broadest accepted sense".
AT	"It is still fresh in my memory that I read a chess book of Karpov by chance in 1985 which I liked very much," the 21-year-old said.
WD	"'Submerged forest'" is a term used to describe the remains of trees (especially tree

[3] These properties are based upon the ostentions of language in Paul Saka's treatment of the use-mention distinction (1998).

	stumps) which have been submerged by marine transgression, i.e. sea level rise.
SY	He also introduced the modern notation for the trigonometric functions, the letter "e" for the base of the natural logarithm (now also known as Euler's number) …
PH	The call of this species is a high pitched "ke-ke-ke" like American Kestrel.
SP	'''James Breckenridge Speed''' (middle name sometimes spelled '''Breckinridge''') (1844-1912) was a successful businessman in Louisville, Kentucky and an important philanthropist.
AB	… "Moskovskiy gosudarstvennyy universitet putej soobshcheniya", often abbreviated '''MIIT''' for '''Moscow Institute of Transport Engineers''' …

Table 2: Examples from the corpus of each category of language-mention. Triple quote marks indicate bold text in the original markup. The longer sentences for SY and AB have been truncated. The relevant instance of language-mention in each example appears underlined.

As shown, proper names were by far the most common category, with almost twice as many instances as the next most frequent category. This follows intuition, since Wikipedia articles often describe entities identified by proper names. In contrast, there were just a few instances of pronunciation (phonetic/sound) or spelling. Either the pre-filtering of sentences eliminated many instances of these before human annotation could find them, or Wikipedia is not a fertile source for them.

Of particular note are the 46 instances of words or phrases as themselves, since these are examples of language being either introduced or clarified for the reader. While there exists a body of work on named entity recognition (Nadeau and Sekine, 2007), very little exists on identifying when words serve a very similar function, essentially as rigid designators for their types. One of the future goals of this project will be to fill that gap.

4 Related Work

A similar corpus-building project was undertaken by Anderson, et. al (2004) to study the occurrence of metalanguage in human dialogue. In addition to the difference in focus (metalanguage broadly versus language-mention in particular), their project concentrated on the classification of utterances from casual speech, as opposed to the structure of well-formed sentences. The automatic recognition of language-mention will require a specific focus on the phenomenon, since it differs from other forms of metalanguage in its unusual syntactic structure (as shown in the next section).

In applications, the use-mention distinction has also received some treatment within dialog management and commonsense reasoning, as implemented in the ALFRED system (Josyula et al., 2003). However, its ability to recognize language-mention is limited to the task of learning new words from a limited set of sentence structures. The ongoing project described in this paper instead has the goal of recognizing and eventually interpreting language-mention in a wide variety of natural cases.

5 Future Work

The next step in this project will be to enlarge the language-mention corpus, using more data from Wikipedia and other promising sources. Language learning materials have also been considered for this purpose, as they necessarily contain a high frequency of metalanguage. The presence of stylistic cues in the text will be useful but perhaps not essential, as it is anticipated that bootstrapping the annotation process will become possible once enough indicators in sentence structure and vocabulary have been identified. This identification will be accomplished through a combination of eyeballing of patterns in parse trees and automated searching through the corpus using a tool such as Tregex (Levy and Andrew, 2006).

One eventual goal of this project is to detect language-mention without the presence of stylistic cues, with the intent of correcting egregious errors common in syntactic parsing of the phenomenon. Statistically-trained parsers have achieved great levels of accuracy at the macro level of examining large quantities of text, but this comes at a cost. Such accuracy tends not to include the phenomenon of language-mention, which often has an unusual structure. Consider the following two sentences paired with the resulting output from the Stanford Parser (Klein and Manning 2003):

(4a) Car is spelled c a r

(4b) (ROOT (S (NP (NNP Car)) (VP (VBZ is) (VP (VBN spelled) (S (NP (SYM c)) (NP (DT a) (NN r)))))))

(5a) The pronunciation of potato is pough tayh toe

(5b) (ROOT (S (NP (NP (DT The) (NN pronunciation)) (PP (IN of) (NP (NN potato)))) (VP (VBZ is) (NP (JJ pough) (NN tayh) (NN toe)))))

Both of these sentences are easily interpretable by a human audience, but the parser garbles their structure where language-mention occurs. Such unusual structure and vocabulary are likely not to lend well to the methods used to train such a parser. Because of this, the feasibility of a "hybrid" system is being investigated, which would combine an existing high-performance parser with a rule-based system to modify and correct its output where appropriate.

Preliminary work on a language-mention parser has shown the feasibility of this hybrid approach. A trial system has been built that uses parse trees produced by the Stanford Parser as input to five rules that detect common syntactic patterns indicating the phenomenon occurs in a sentence. In (4a), for instance, the presence of the verb *spell* and the sequence of two or more single-letter words indicates that the sequence is likely an instance of language-mention and falls into the category of spelling. Although language-mention exhibits substantial variety in its forms (and certainly will not be conquered by the five rules in the trial system), this approach should be able to take advantage of additional patterns mined from the corpus of the phenomenon currently being created. It is hypothesized that such a parser, using lexical and syntactic cues, will be sufficient to identify and categorize a large percentage of instances of language-mention in the absence of any stylistic cues.

References

Anderson, Michael L., Andrew Fister, Bryant Lee, and Danny Wang. 2004. On the frequency and types of meta-language in conversation: a preliminary report. Paper presented at the 14th Annual Conference of the Society for Text and Discourse.

Anderson, Michael L., Yoshi Okamoto, Darsana Josyula, and Don Perlis. 2002. The use-mention distinction and its importance to HCI. In *Proceedings of the Sixth Workshop on the Semantics and Pragmatics of Dialog*.

Josyula, Darsana, Mike Anderson, and Don Perlis. 2003. Towards domain-independent, task-oriented, conversational adequacy. In *Proceedings of IJCAI-2003 Intelligent Systems Demonstrations*.

Kiss, Tibor and Jan Strunk. 2006. Unsupervised multilingual sentence boundary detection. *Computational Linguistics,* 32(4): 485-525.

Klein, Dan and Christopher Manning. 2003. Accurate Unlexicalized Parsing. In *Proceedings of the 41st Meeting of the Association for Computational Linguistics*.

Levy, Roger and Galen Andrew. 2006. Tregex and Tsurgeon: tools for querying and manipulating tree data structures. In *Proceedings of the 8th International Conference on Knowledge-Based Intelligent Information and Engineering Systems*.

Maier, Emar. 2007. Mixed quotation: between use and mention. In *Proceedings of LENLS2007*, Miyazaki, Japan.

Miller, Michael. 1993. A view of one's past and other aspects of reasoned change in belief. Ph.D. thesis, University of Maryland, College Park, Maryland.

Nadeau, David and Satoshi Sekine. 2007. A survey of named entity recognition and classification. *Linguisticae Investigationes*, 30(1):3–26.

Perlis, Don, Khemdut Purang, and Carl Andersen. 1998. Conversational adequacy: mistakes are the essence. *International Journal of Human-Computer Studies,* 48:553-575.

Saka, Paul. 1998. Quotation and the use-mention distinction. *Mind,* 107(425):113–135.

Saka, Paul. 2005. Quotational constructions. *Belgian Journal of Linguistics,* 17(1):187–212.

Snow, Rion, Brendan O'Connor, Daniel Jurafsky, and Andrew Y. Ng. Cheap and fast—but is it good? Evaluating non-expert annotations for natural language tasks. 2008. In *Proceedings of the Conference on Empirical Methods in Natural Language Processing*. Honolulu, Hawaii.

A Learning-based Sampling Approach to Extractive Summarization

Vishal Juneja and Sebastian Germesin and Thomas Kleinbauer
German Research Center for Artificial Intelligence
Campus D3.2
66123 Saarbücken, Germany
{firstname.lastname}@dfki.de

Abstract

In this paper we present a novel resampling model for extractive meeting summarization. With resampling based on the output of a baseline classifier, our method outperforms previous research in the field. Further, we compare an existing resampling technique with our model. We report on an extensive series of experiments on a large meeting corpus which leads to classification improvement in weighted precision and f-score.

1 Introduction

Feature-based machine learning approaches have become a standard technique in the field of extractive summarization wherein the most important sections within a meeting transcripts need to be identified. We perceive the problem as recognizing the most extract-worthy meeting dialog acts (DAs) in a binary classification framework.

In this paper, firstly, in section 4 we create a *gold standard* to train the classifier, by improvising upon the existing annotations in our meeting corpus. Then in section 5 we present actual numbers which display a very skewed class distribution to learn for the binary classifier. This skewness is attributed to the less number of actual extract-worthy and important DAs (positive examples) compared to ordinary chit-chat, backchannel noises etc (negative examples) spoken during the course of the meeting. We tackle this data skewness with a novel resampling approach which reselects the data set to create a more comparable class distribution between these postive and negative instances.

Resampling methods have been found effective in catering to the data imbalance problem mentioned above. (Corbett and Copestake, 2008) used a resampling module for chemical named entity recognition. The pre-classifier, based on n-gram character features, assigned a probability of being a chemical word, to each token. Only tokens having probability greater than a predefined threshold were preserved and the output of the first stage classification along with word suffix were used as features in further classification steps. (Hinrichs et al., 2005) used a hybrid approach for Computational Anaphora Resolution (CAR) combining rule based filtering with Memory based learning to reduce the huge population of anaphora/candidate-antecedent pairs. (Xie et al., 2008), in their experimentation on the ICSI meeting corpus, employ the salience scores generated by a TFIDF classifier in the resampling task. We discuss the actual technique and our resampling module further in section 6.

We compare its performance with the TFIDF model of (Xie et al., 2008) in section 8.2 and observe a general improvement in summary scores through resampling.

2 Data

We use the scenario meetings of the AMI corpus for our experiments in this paper which comprise about two thirds of around 100 hours of recorded and annotated meetings. The scenario meetings each have four participants who play different roles in a fictitious company for designing a remote control. The AMI corpus has a standard training set of 94

Proceedings of the NAACL HLT 2010 Student Research Workshop, pages 34–39,
Los Angeles, California, June 2010.

meetings[1] and 20 meetings each for development and testing.

Annotators wrote abstractive summaries for each meeting and then linked summary sentences to those DA segments from the meeting transcripts which best conveyed the information in the abstracts. There was no limit on the number of links an annotator could create and a many-to-many mapping exists between the meeting DA segments and human abstracts. Here, DA segments are used in analogy to sentences in document summarization because the spontaneously spoken material in meeting transcripts rarely contains actual grammatical sentences.

3 Pre-processing and Feature Extraction

To the feature set of (Murray, 2008) listed in table 1 we add some high level features. Since the main focus of this paper is to deal with the data imbalanace issue hence for the sake of completeness and reproducibility of our work we briefly mention the basic features used. In section 8.3 we explicitly report the performance rise over the baseline due to the added features.

3.1 Lexical and Structural features

The list of added features include the number of content words (nouns and adjectives) in a DA. (Edmundson, 1969) looked at cue-phrases, keywords title and location of a sentence as features indicative of important sections in a document. We use a handpicked list of cue words like "for example", "gonna have" etc as binary features. We also add several keywords like "remote","plastic" etc based upon manual scrutiny, as binary features into the classifier. Further we use DA labels of current and four adjacent DAs as features.

3.2 Disfluency

The role of disfluencies in summarization has been investigated by (Zhu and Penn, 2006) before. They found that disfluencies improve summarization performance when used as an additional feature. We count the number of disfluent words in a DA using an automatic disfluency detector.

[1]Three of the meetings were missing some required features.

3.3 Prosodic

We employ all the signal level features described by (Murray, 2008) which include mean, max and standard deviation of energy and pitch values normalized by both speaker and meeting. The duration of the DA in terms of time and number of words spoken. The subsequent, precedent pauses and rate of speech feature.

DA Features
mean energy
mean pitch
maximum energy value
maximum pitch value
standard deviation of pitch
precedent pause
subsequent pause
uninterrupted length
number of words
position in the meeting
position in the speaker turn
DA time duration
speaker dominance in DA
speaker dominance in time
rate of speech
SUIDF score
TFIDF score

Table 1: Features used in baseline classifier

4 Gold Standard

In supervised frameworks, the creation of *gold-standard* annotations for training (and testing) is known to be a difficult task, since (a) what should go into a summary can be a matter of opinion and (b) multiple sentences from the original document may express similar content, making each of them equally good candidates for selection. The hypothesis is well supported by the low *kappa* value (Cohen, 1960) of 0.48 reported by (Murray, 2008) on the AMI corpus.

We describe the procedure for creating the gold standard for our experimentation in this paper. Firstly we join all annotations and rank the DAs from most number of links to least number of links to create a sorted list of DAs. Depending on a predefined variable percentage as gold standard cut-off or threshold we preserve the corresponding number of highest ranked DAs in the above list. For evaluation, (Murray, 2008) uses gold standard summaries obtained using similar procedure. For training, however, he uses all DA segments with at least one link as positive examples.

As the term gold standard for the data set, created above, is misleading. We call the set of DAs so obtained by using this ranking and resampling procedure as Weighted-Resampled Gold Standard (WRGS). Henceforth in this paper, for a resampling rate of say 35% we will name the set of DAs so obtained as WRGS(35%) or simply WRGS for some undefined, arbitrary threshold.

5 Data Skewness

In this section we focus on the skewed data set which arises because of creating WRGS for training our classifiers. Consider the set of DAs with at least one link to the abstractive or human summaries. Let us call it $DA^{l \geq 1}$. This set accounts for 20.9% of all DAs in the training set.

set	size%
WRGS(25%)	5.22%
$DA^{l \geq 1}$	20.9%

Table 2: Set sizes in % of all training DAs

Again consider set of DAs for WRGS(25%). This set, by definition, contains 25% of all DAs in the set $DA^{l \geq 1}$. Hence the set WRGS(25%) constitute 5.22% of all DAs in the training set. Note that this is a skewed class distribution as also visible in table 2.

Our system employs resampling architecture shown in figure 1. The first classifier is similar in spirit to the one developed in (Murray, 2008) with the additional features listed in section 3. The output we use is not the discrete classification result but rather the probability for each DA segment to be extracted.

These probabilities are used in two ways for training the second classifier: firstly, to create the resampled training set and secondly, as an additional feature for the second classifier. The procedure for resampling is explained in the section 6.

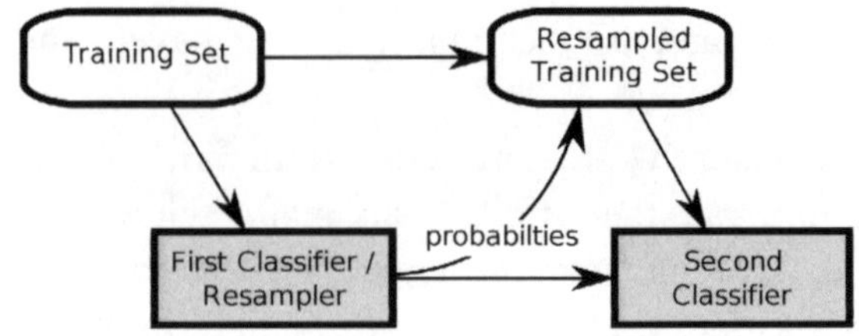

Figure 1: A two-step classification architecture for extractive meeting summarization.

6 Resampling

As explained in previous section our model obtains resampled data for second stage classification using the probabilistic outcomes of a first stage classifier. The resampling is done similar to (Xie et al., 2008) to cater to the data skewness problem. To do the resampling, firstly, the DAs are ranked on decreasing probabilities. In the next step, depending on some resampling rate, a percentage of highest ranked DAs is used in further classification steps, while rest of DA segments are neglected.

(Xie et al., 2008) obtained the resampled set by ranking the DAs on TFIDF weights. Data resampling benefits the model in two ways a) by improving the positive/negative example ratio during the training phase b) by discarding noisy utterances in the test phase as they usually attain low scores from the first classifier.

In testing, the first classifier is run on the test data, its output is used, as in training, to create the resampled test set and the probability features. Finally, the summary is created from the probabilities produced by the second classifier by selecting the highest ranked DA segments for the specified summary length.

As the data for resampling is derived by a learning-based classifier, we call our approach *Learning-Based Sampling* (LBS).

In this paper, we compare our LBS model with the TFIDF sampling approach adopted by (Xie et al., 2008) and present the results of resampling on both models in section 8.2.

For comparison, we use Murray's (2008) state of art extractive summarization model.

7 Evaluation Metric

The main metric we use for evaluating the summaries is the extension of the *weighted precision* evaluation scheme introduced by (Murray, 2008). The measure relies on having multiple annotations for a meeting and a many-to-many mapping discussed in section 2. To calculate weighted precision, the number of times that each extractive summary DA was linked by each annotator is counted and averaged to get a single DA score. The DA scores are then averaged over all DAs in the summary to get the weighted precision score for the entire summary. The total number of links in an extractive summary divided by the total number of links to the abstract as a whole gives the weighted recall score. By this definition, weighted recall can have a maximum score of 1 since it is a fraction of the total links for the entire summary. Also, there is no theoretical maximum for weighted precision as annotators were allowed to create any number of links for a single DA.

Both weighted precision and recall share the same numerator: $num = \Sigma_d L_d/N$ where L_d is the number of links for a DA d in the extractive summary, and N is the number of annotators. Weighted precision is equal to $wp = num/D_s$ where D_s is the number of DAs in the extractive summary. Weighted recall is given by $recall = num/(L_t/N)$ where L_t is the total number of links made between DAs and abstract sentences by all annotators, and N is the number of annotators. The f-score is calculated as: $(2 \times wp \times recall)/(wp + recall)$.

In simple terms a DA which might be discussing an important meeting topic e.g. selling price of the remote control etc is more likely to be linked by more than one annotator and possibly more than once by an annotator. Therefore the high scoring DAs are in a way indicative of quintessential topics and agenda points of the meeting. Hence, weighted precision which is number of links per annotator averaged over all the meeting DAs is a figure that aligns itself with average information content per DA in the summary. Low scoring meeting chit-chats will tend to bring the precision score down. We report a weighted precision of 1.33 for 700 word summary extracted using the procedure described in 2 for obtaining gold standard. This is hence a ceiling to the weighted precision score that can be obtained by any summary corresponding to this compression rate. Weighted Recall on the other hand signifies total information content of the meeting. For intelligent systems in general the recall rate increases with increasing summary compression rates while weighted precision decreases[2].

Since we experiment with short summaries that have at most 700 words, we do most of the comparisons in terms of weighted precision values. In the final system evaluation in section 8.3, we include weighted recall and f-score values.

8 Experimental Results and Discussion

8.1 Training on gold standard

Figure 2 shows the weighted precision results on training an SVM classifier with different gold standard thresholds. For example, at a threshold of 60%, the top 60% of the linked DA segments are defined as the gold standard positive examples, all other DA segments of the meeting are defined as negative, non-extraction worthy. The tests are performed on a single stage classifier similar to (Murray, 2008).

In addition, the curves show the behavior of the system at three different summary compression rates (i.e., number of words in the summary). A general tendency that can be observed is the increase in summary scores with decreasing threshold. For 700 word summaries the peak weighted precision score is observed at 35% threshold. The recall rate remains constant as seen by comparing the first two rows of table 5.

We believe that low inter annotator agreement is the major factor responsible for these results. This shows that a reduced subset classification approach will generally improve results when multiple annotations are available.

8.2 Resampling

In this section we compare two resampling models. The TFIDF model explained in section 6 selects best DAs based on their TFIDF scores. As discussed

[2] An important point to notice is that, a high recall rate does not ensure a good content coverage by the summary. As an example, the summary might pick up DAs pertaining to only a few very important points discussed during the meeting which will lead to a high recall rate although lesser important concepts may still be exclusive.

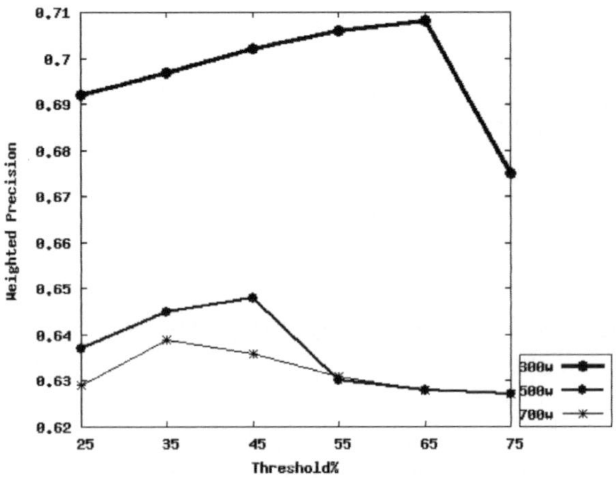

Figure 2: SVM at different compression rates.

previously all sentences above a resampling threshold are preserved while rest are discarded. In 8.2.2 resampling is done from the probabilities of a first stage classifier. SVM model is used for both first and second stage classification.

8.2.1 TFIDF Resampling

Table 3 reports weighted precision and f-scores at two compression rates. The highest f-scores for 700, 1000 word summaries are obtained at 85% and 55% respectively. Plots of figure 3 compare weighted precision scores for LBS and TFIDF models.

# words:	700		1000	
resampl. %	wp	f-score	wp	f-score
15	.631	.217	.600	.274
25	.670	.227	.610	.282
35	.673	.227	.630	.296
55	.685	.231	**.641**	**.305**
75	.689	.232	.632	.302
85	**.692**	**.233**	.631	.299
100	.686	.231	.637	.302

Table 3: TFIDF weighted Precision, f-score for 700 and 1000 word summaries

8.2.2 LBS

The peak performance of the LBS model is observed at resampling rate of 35% for both 700 and 1000 word summaries as seen in table 4. The maximum f-scores, 0.248 and 0.319 (table 4) obtained for LBS outperforms maximum f-scores of 0.233 and 0.305 (table 3) for TFIDF.

# words:	700		1000	
resampl. %	wp	f-score	wp	f-score
15	.684	.236	.662	.309
25	.706	.244	.664	.317
35	**.710**	**.248**	**.664**	**.319**
55	.707	.245	.652	.313
75	.702	.239	.650	.310
85	.702	.239	.642	.307
100	.692	.236	.639	.306

Table 4: weighted precision, f-scores on LBS model

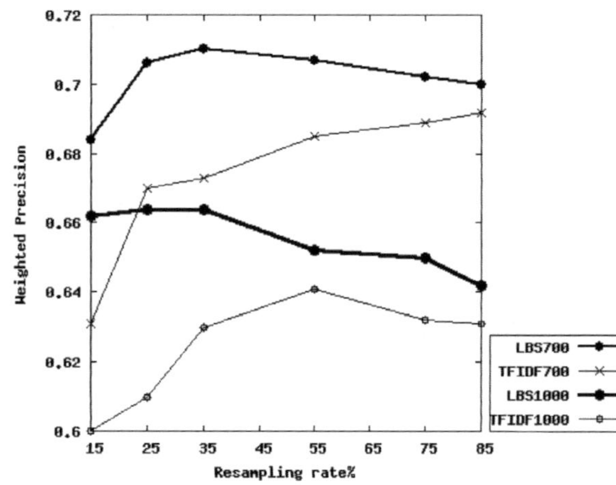

Figure 3: LBS and TFIDF wp values at different compression rates.

From figure 4 which shows positive example retention against sampling rate for TFIDF and LBS it is clear that for all sampling rates, LBS provides a higher rate of positive examples.

Also as discussed above, using a learning-based first classifier produces probability values that can be leveraged as features for the second classifier. We speculate that this also contributes to the differences in overall performance.

8.3 Overall System Performance

In this section we report weighted precision, recall and f-score for 700-word summaries, comparing results of the new model with the initial baseline system.

As shown in table 5, training the system on

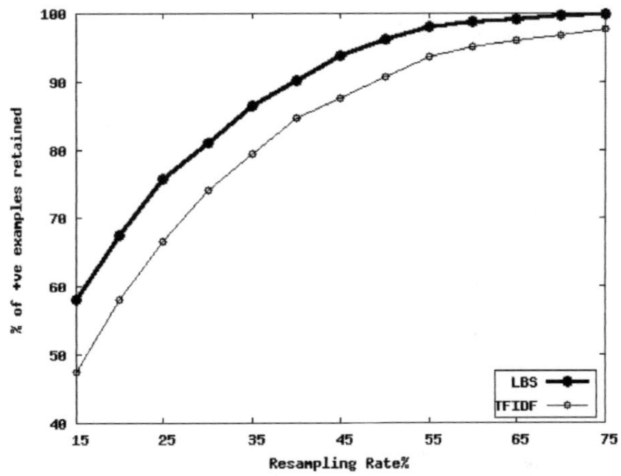

Figure 4: LBS and TFIDF retention rates.

WRGS, with a threshold of 35% increases the precision score from 0.61 to 0.64 while maintaining the recall rate. This is corresponding to the weighted precision score for 35% data point in figure 2.

The last row in table 5 correspond to results obtained with using the LBS proposed in this paper. The scores at 35% resampling are same as the bold faced observations in table 4 for 700 word summaries. We observe that the LBS architecture alone brings about an absolute improvement of 4.41% and 8.69% in weighted precision and f-score.

System	wp	recall	f-score
baseline	0.61	0.13	0.20
+ gold standard	0.64	0.13	0.20
+ new features	0.68	0.15	0.23
+ resampling(LBS 35)%	0.71	0.16	0.25

Table 5: Results on the AMI corpus.

9 Conclusions and Future Work

Through our experimental results in this paper, we firstly observed that training the classifier on WRGS (weighted-resampled gold standard) instances, rather than all the annotated DAs improved the weighted precision scores of our summarizer. We further addressed the problem of skewed class distribution in our data set and introduced a learning-based resampling approach where we resample from the probabilistic outcomes of a first stage classifier. We noted that resampling the data set increased performance, peaking at around 35% sampling rate. We compared the LBS model with the TFIDF resampler obtaining better f-scores from our proposed machine learning based architecture. We conclude in general that resampling techniques for resolving data imbalance problem in extractive meeting summarization domain, results in enhanced system performance.

We are currently working on multiple extensions of this work, including investigating how the results can be applied to other corpora, adding additional features, and finally methods for post-processing extractive summaries.

Acknowledgments This work is supported by the European IST Programme Project AMIDA [FP6-0033812]. This paper only reflects the authors views and funding agencies are not liable for any use that may be made of the information contained herein.

References

Jacob Cohen. 1960. A coefficient of agreement for nominal scales. In *Educational and Psychological Measurement*.

Peter Corbett and Ann Copestake. 2008. Cascaded classifiers for confidence-based chemical named entity recognition. In *Current Trends in Biomedical Natural Language Processing*.

H. P. Edmundson. 1969. New methods in automatic extracting. In *J. ACM, 16(2)*.

Erhard W. Hinrichs, Katja Filippova, and HolgerWunsch. 2005. A data-driven approach to pronominal anaphora resolution for german. In *In Proceedings of Recent Advances in Natural Language Processing*.

Gabriel Murray. 2008. *Using Speech-Specific Characteristics for Automatic Speech Summarization*. Ph.D. thesis, University of Edinburgh.

Shasha Xie, Yang Liu, and Hui Lin. 2008. Evaluating the effectiveness of features and sampling in extractive meeting summarization. In *IEEE Spoken Language Technology Workshop (SLT)*, pages 157–160.

Xiaodan Zhu and Gerald Penn. 2006. Summarization of spontaneous conversations. In *Proceedings of the 2006 ACM Conference on Computer Supported Cooperative Work (CSCW 2006),*.

Temporal Relation Identification with Endpoints

Chong Min Lee
Georgetown University
3700 O Street, NW
Washington, D.C. 20057, USA
cml54@georgetown.edu

Abstract

Temporal relation classification task has issues of fourteen target relations, skewed distribution of the target relations, and relatively small amount of data. To overcome the issues, methods such as merging target relations and increasing data size with closure algorithm have been used. However, the method using merged relations has a problem on how to recover original relations. In this paper, a new reduced-relation method is proposed. The method decomposes a target relation into four pairs of endpoints with three target relations. After classifying a relation of each endpoint pair, four classified relations are combined into a relation of original fourteen target relations. In the combining step, two heuristics are examined.

1 Introduction

An interesting task in temporal information processing is how to identify a temporal relation between a pair of temporal entities such as events (EVENT) and time expressions (TIMEX) in a narrative. After the publication of TimeBank (Pustejovsky et al., 2003b) annotated in TimeML (Pustejovsky et al., 2003a), supervised learning techniques have been tested in the temporal relation identification task with different types of temporal entity pairs (Chambers et al., 2007; Boguraev and Ando, 2005; Verhagen et al., 2007).

There are three issues in applying supervised machine learning methods to this task. The first issue is that a temporal entity pair that is defined as a directed temporal link (TLINK) in TimeML should be classified into a relation among fourteen relations. The second issue is that the number of TLINKs is relatively small in spite of the fourteen targets. The third issue is skewed distributions of the relations. Without the solutions of the issues, it is impossible to achieve good performance in temporal relation identification through machine learning techniques.

Several solutions have been suggested such as increased number of TLINKs with a transitivity closure algorithm (Mani et al., 2007; Chambers et al., 2007) and decreased target relations into six (Mani et al., 2006; Chambers et al., 2007; Tatu and Srikanth, 2008) or three (Verhagen et al., 2007). An issue of the reduced-relation method is how to recover original relations. A module for the recovery can cause performance degeneration and seems intuitively inappropriate.

In this paper, a new reduced-relation method is presented. The method uses endpoints of temporal entities. A TimeML relation can be represented into four endpoint pairs with three relations: *before, equal,* and *after*. This method requires four relation identification classifiers among endpoints for a TLINK and each classifier has only three target relations instead of fourteen. The four classified relations need to be combined in order to restore an interval-based relation. In this study, the performance of the proposed method will be evaluated in identifying TLINK relations between temporal entities empirically.

Firstly, related studies are described in section 2. Secondly, the identification of four pointwise relations is described. Thirdly, methods for the combination of pointwise relations are explained. Finally,

Proceedings of the NAACL HLT 2010 Student Research Workshop, pages 40–45,
Los Angeles, California, June 2010.

the outlook of the proposed method is proposed.

2 Background

Temporal relation identification has three problems: sparse data, fourteen target relations, and skewed distribution. To reduce the problems, previous studies have used techniques such as increasing data size with closure algorithm and merging target relations.

Mani et al. (2006) used closure algorithm to increase training data size and merged inverse relations into six main relations. Their study applied the methods to classify relations of all TLINKs and showed the benefit of the methods in temporal relation identification. Chambers et al. (2007) reported 67.0% accuracy on the relation identification task among EVENT-EVENT (EE) TLINKs using the merged relations. And, the accuracy is the best performance with EE TLINKs.

The merging method assumes that target relations of TLINKs is already known. When a TLINK relation from an anchor to a target is *AFTER*, it can be changed into *BEFORE* by conversing the anchor and the target each other. When unknown instance is given, the merging process is impossible. When six merged relations were used as target relations, we assumes the conversion is already done. And the assumption is inappropriate.

TempEval07 (Verhagen et al., 2007) integrated 14 TLINK relations into three: *before*, *after*, and *overlap*. *overlap* is an extended relation that covers 12 relations except *BEFORE* and *AFTER*. This approach has a burden to recover 12 relations from the extensive one.

In this study, a TLINK is decomposed into four pairs of endpoint links in the step of applying machine learning approaches. Then, four classified endpoint relations are combined into a TimeML relation. Allen (1983) showed a relative order between intervals can be decomposed into relative orders of four endpoint pairs. In TimeML, temporal entities, EVENT and TIMEX, are intervals. An interval has a pair of endpoints: start and end. A relation between two intervals can be represented into relations of four pairs of starts and ends as in Table 2. A relative order between endpoints can be represented with three relations: *before*, *equal*, and *after*. The proposed method will be empirically investigated in this study.

3 Resources and Data Preparation

3.1 Temporal Corpora

TimeBank and Opinion corpora consist of 183 and 73 documents respectively. Among the documents, it is found that 42 documents have inconsistent TLINKs. The inconsistencies make it impossible to apply closure algorithm to the documents. Therefore, the 42 documents with inconsistent TLINKs are excluded. This study focuses on classifying relations of three types of TLINKs: TLINKs between EVENTs (EE), between an EVENT and a TIMEX (ET), and between an EVENT and Document Creation Time (ED).

As a preparation step, fourteen relations are merged into eleven relations (TimeML relations). *SIMULTANEOUS, IDENTITY, DURING,* and *DURUNG_BY* relations are identical in relative order between entities. Therfore, the relations are integrated into SIMULTANEOUS[1]. Then, closure algorithm is run on the documents to increase the number of TLINKs. The distribution of relations of three types is given in Table 1.

A document with merged relations is divided into four documents with endpoint relations: start of anchor and start of target, start of anchor and end of target, end of anchor and start of target, and end of anchor and end of target documents. The conversion table of a TimeML relation into four endpoint relations is given in Table 2 and the distribution of three relations after the conversion is given in 3.

4 Relation identification with end points

In endpoint relation identification experiment, support vector machine (SVM) and maximum entropy classifiers are built to classify three relations: *before, equal,* and *after*. First, feature vectors are constructed. When four endpoint links are from a TLINK, their feature vectors are identical except target endpoint relations.

[1] Mani et al. (2006) said DURING was merged into IS_INCLUSED. However, DURING, SIMULTANEOUS, and IDENTITY are converted into = of Allen's relations in `Tarski Toolkit` (Verhagen et al., 2005). In this paper, the implementation is followed.

Relation	EVENT-EVENT		EVENT-TIMEX		EVENT-DCT	
	Original	Closed	Original	Closed	Original	Closed
AFTER	735	11083	86	2016	169	259
BEFORE	1239	12445	160	1603	721	1291
BEGINS	35	75	23	36	0	0
BEGUN_BY	38	74	51	58	10	11
ENDS	15	64	65	128	0	0
ENDED_BY	87	132	43	61	6	6
IAFTER	38	138	3	8	1	1
IBEFORE	49	132	2	9	0	0
INCLUDES	246	3987	122	166	417	469
IS_INCLUDED	327	4360	1495	2741	435	467
SIMULTANEOUS	1370	2348	201	321	75	90

Table 1: Distribution of TimeML relations

TimeML Relation	**Inverse**	**Endpoint Relations**
x BEFORE y	y AFTER x	$x^- < y^-, x^- < y^+,$ $x^+ < y^-, x^+ < y^+$
x SIMULTANEOUS y	y SIMULTANEOUS x	$x^- = y^-, x^- < y^+,$ $x^+ > y^-, x^+ = y^+$
x IBEFORE y	y IAFTER x	$x^- < y^-, x^- < y^+,$ $x^+ = y^-, x^+ < y^+$
x BEGINS y	y BEGUN_BY x	$x^- = y^-, x^- < y^+,$ $x^+ > y^-, x^+ < y^+$
x ENDS y	y ENDED_BY x	$x^- > y^-, x^- < y^+,$ $x^+ > y^-, x^+ = y^+$
x INCLUDES y	y IS_INCLUDED x	$x^- < y^-, x^- < y^+,$ $x^+ > y^-, x^+ > y^+$

Table 2: Relation conversion table

End pairs	EVENT-EVENT			EVENT-TIMEX			EVENT-DCT		
	before	*equal*	*after*	*before*	*equal*	*after*	*before*	*equal*	*after*
start-start	1621 (39%)	1443 (35%)	1115 (27%)	327 (15%)	275 (12%)	1649 (73%)	1144 (62%)	85 (5%)	605 (33%)
start-end	3406 (82%)	38 (1%)	735 (18%)	2162 (**96%**)	3	86 (4%)	1664 (**91%**)	1	169 (9%)
end-start	1239 (30%)	49 (1%)	2891 (69%)	160 (7%)	2	2089 (**93%**)	721 (39%)	0	1113 (61%)
end-end	1650 (39%)	1472 (35%)	1057 (25%)	1680 (75%)	309 (14%)	262 (12%)	1156 (63%)	81 (4%)	597 (33%)

Table 3: Distribution of end point relations.

10-fold cross validation is applied at document-level. In some previous studies, all temporal links were collected into a set and the set was split into training and test data without the distinction on sources. However, the approach could boost system performance as shown in Tatu and Srikanth (2008).

When TLINKs in a file are split in training and test data, links in training data can be composed of similar words in test data. In that case, the links in training can play a role of background knowledge. Therefore, document-level 10-fold cross validation is exploited.

4.1 Features

In constructing feature vectors of three TLINK types, features that were used in order to identify TimeML relations in previous studies are adopted. The features have been proved useful in identifying a TimeML relation in the studies. Moreover, the features still seem helpful for endpoint relation identification task. For example, *past* and *present* tenses of two EVENTs could be a clue to make a prediction that *present* tensed EVENT is probably after *past* tensed EVENT.

Annotated information of EVENT and TIMEX in the temporal corpora is used in the feature vector construction. This proposed approach to use end-point conversion in relation identification task is the first attempt. Therefore, the annotated values are used as features in order to see the effect of this approach. However, state-of-the-arts natural language processing programs such as Charniak parser and Porter Stemmer are sometimes used to extract additional features such as stems of event words, the existence of both entities in the same phrase, and etc.

> The company has ***reported declines*** in operating profit in ***the past three years***

Features for EVENT TENSE, ASPECT, MODAL, POS, and CLASS annotations are borrowed from temporal corpora as features. And, a stem of an EVENT word is added as a feature instead of a word itself in order to normalize it. *reported* is represented as <(TENSE:present), (ASPECT:perferce), (MODAL:none), (POS: verb), (CLASS: reporting), (STEM:report)>.

Features for TIMEX In the extraction of TIMEX features, it tries to capture if specific words are in a time expression to normalize temporal expressions. The time point of an expression can be inferred through the specific words such as *ago, coming, current, earlier* and etc. Additionally, the existence of plural words such as *seconds, minutes, hours, days, months,* and *years* is added as a feature. The specific words are:

- *ago, coming, current, currently, earlier, early, every, following, future, last, later, latest, next, now, once, past, previously, recent, recently, soon, that, the, then, these, this, today, tomorrow, within, yesterday,* and *yet*

the past three years are represented as <(AGO:0), (COMING:0), (CURRENT:0), (CURRENTLY:0), (EARLIER:0), (EARLY:0), (EVERY:0), (FOLLOWING:0), (FUTURE:0), (LAST:1), (LATER:0), (LASTED:0), (NEXT:0), (NOW:0), (ONCE:0), (PAST:1), (PREVIOUSLY:0), (RECENT:0), (RECENTLY:0), (SOON:0), (THAT:0), (THE:1), (THEN:0), (THESE:0), (THIS:0), (TODAY:0), (TOMORRWO:0), (WITHIN:0), (YESTERDAY:0), (YET:0), (PLURAL:1)>.

Relational features between entities In addition, relational information between two entities is used as features. It is represented if two entities are in the same sentence. To get the other relational information, a sentence is parsed with Charniak parser. Syntactic path from an anchor to a target is calculated from the parsed tree. A syntactic path from *reported* to *the past three years* is "VBN||VP||PP||NP". It is represented if two entities are in the same phrase and clause with the path. When only one clause or phrase exists in the path except part-of-speeches of both entities, the features are marked as 1s. The counts of words, phrases, and clauses between temporal entities are also used as features. When two entities are not in the same sentence, 0s are given as the values of the features except the word count. Some prepositions and conjunctions are used as features when the words are used as a head word of syntactic path from an entity to the other entity. In the example of "VBN||VP||PP||NP", "in" in "in the past three years" is the head word of PP. So, *in* is marked 1. The head words that are used as features are:

- *after, as, at, before, between, by, during, for, in, once, on, over, since, then, through, throughout, until, when,* and *while*

EE and ET types have feature vectors that consist of features of both entities and relational features. ED type has only features of EVENT.

5 Restoration of original relations

Four endpoint relations of a TLINK are classified in the previous section. The combination of the classified relations needs to be restored into a relation among the eleven merged TimeML relations. However, due to the independence of four classifiers, it is not guaranteed that a TimeML relation can be generated from four endpoint relations. When the restoration fails, the existence of errors in the four predictions is implied. In this step, two methods to restore a TimeML relation are investigated: Minimum Edit Distance (MED) and Highest Score (HS).

MED checks how many substitutions are needed to restore a TimeML relation. A TimeML relation with the minimum changes is defined as the restored relation. Let's suppose four endpoint relations are given such as x^- *before* y^-, x^- *after* y^+, x^+ *before* y^-, and x^+ *before* y^+. Among other possible ways to get a TimeML relation, *BEFORE* could be recovered with a change of *before* in x^- *after* y^+ into *before*. Therefore, *BEFORE* is chosen as a restored TimeML relation. When several candidates are available, a method is examined in selecting one. The method is to give weight on classifiers that show better performance. If two candidates are available by changing *before* of start-start or *before* of start-end in ET type, this method selects a candidate by changing *before* when *before* of start-end shows better performance.

HS uses the sum of confidence scores from classifiers. Each classifier of the four endpoint pairs generates confidence scores of three relations (*before*, *equal*, and *after*). Among 81 possible combinations of four classifiers with three target relations, the highest-scored one that can be restored into a TimeML relation is chosen as a prediction. When several candidates exist, the selection method of MED is also adopted.

6 Expectations and future plans

First, I will show how beneficial four endpoint systems are at identifying endpoint relations. F-measure will be used to show the performance of an endpoint relation classifier in identifying each endpoint relation. And, accuracy is used to report overall performance of the classifier. Second, I will show how effective the endpoint method is in identifying TLINK relations. I will build a base classifier with eleven TimeML relations and feature vectors that are identical with the endpoint systems. The performance difference in identifying TimeML relations between this proposed system and the base system will be presented to show whether this proposed approach is successful.

Previous research such as Verhagen et al. (2007) using three reltions as target relations showed from 60% to 80% performance according to TLINK types. Moreover, some distributions of endpoint relations show over 90% such as *before* of end-start in ET and ED TLINKs, and *after* of end-start in ET TLINK in Table 3. Therefore, we can expect each endpoint identification system will perform well in classifying endpoint relations.

The success of this new approach will depend on the restoration step. The excessively skewed distributions can make similar predicted sequences of endpoint relations. It can weaken the advantage of this endpoint approach that every TimeML relation can be generated through combining endpoint relations. For example, *equal* shows very small distributions in start-end and end-start endpoint pairs. Therefore, it is probable that TimeML relations such as *IAFTER* and *IBEFORE* cannot be classified correctly. It can be a challenge how to correctly classify endpoint relations with small distribution.

One possible solution for the challenge is to check global consistency among classified relations such as Bramsen et al. (2006) and Chambers and Jurafsky (2008). The global consistency restoration can give a chance to replace excessively distributed relations with sparse relations. However, *equal* is used additionally in this study. Therefore, modifications in the method of Bramsen et al. (2006) and Chambers and Jurafsky (2008) are needed before applying their method.

References

James Allen. 1983. Maintaining knowledge about temporal intervals. *Communications of the Association for Computing Machinery*, 26(1):832–843.

Branimir Boguraev and Rie Kubota Ando. 2005. TimeML-compliant text analysis for temporal reasoning. In *Proceedings of the 2005 International Joint Conference on Artificial Intelligence*, pages 997–1003.

Philip Bramsen, Pawan Deshpande, Yoong Keok Lee, and Regina Barzilay. 2006. Inducing temporal graphs. In *Proceedings of the 2006 Conference on Empirical Methods on Natural Language Processing*, pages 189–198.

Nathanael Chambers and Dan Jurafsky. 2008. Jointly combining implicit constraints improves temporal ordering. In *EMNLP '08: Proceedings of the Conference on Empirical Methods in Natural Language Processing*, pages 698–706, Morristown, NJ, USA. Association for Computational Linguistics.

Nathanael Chambers, Shan Wang, and Dan Jurafsky. 2007. Classifying temporal relations between events. In *Proceedings of 45th Annual Meeting of the Association for Computational Linguistics*, pages 173–176.

Inderjeet Mani, Marc Verhagen, Ben Wellner, Chong Min Lee, and James Pustejovsky. 2006. Machine learning of temporal relations. In *Proceedings of the 21st International Conference on Computational Linguistics and 44th Annual Meeting of the Association for Computational Linguistics*.

Inderjeet Mani, Ben Wellner, Marc Verhagen, and James Pustejovsky. 2007. Three approaches to learning tlinks in timeml. Technical Report CS-07-268, Brandeis University, Waltham, MA, USA.

James Pustejovsky, Jose Castao, Robert Ingria, Roser Saur, Robert Gaizauskas, and Andrea Setzer. 2003a. TimeML: robust specification of event and temporal expressions in text. In *IWCS-5 Fifth International Workshop on Computational Semantics*.

James Pustejovsky, Patrick Hanks, Roser Saur, Andrew See, David Day, Lisa Ferro, Robert Gaizauskas, Marcia Lazo, Andrea Setzer, and Beth Sundheim. 2003b. The TimeBank corpus. In *Proceedings of Corpus Linguistics 2003*, pages 647–656, Lancaster, UK.

Marta Tatu and Munirathnam Srikanth. 2008. Experiments with reasoning for temporal relations between events. In *COLING '08: Proceedings of the 22nd International Conference on Computational Linguistics*, pages 857–864, Morristown, NJ, USA. Association for Computational Linguistics.

Marc Verhagen, Inderjeet Mani, Roser Sauri, Robert Knippen, Seok Bae Jang, Jessica Littman, Anna Rumshisky, John Phillips, and James Pustejovsky. 2005. Automating temporal annotation with tarsqi. In *ACL '05: Proceedings of the ACL 2005 on Interactive poster and demonstration sessions*, pages 81–84, Morristown, NJ, USA. Association for Computational Linguistics.

Marc Verhagen, Robert Gaizauskas, Frank Schilder, Mark Hepple, Graham Katz, and James Pustejovsky. 2007. SemEval-2007 task 15: TempEval temporal relation identification. In *Proceedings of the 4th International Workshop on Semantic Evaluations (SemEval-2007)*, pages 75–80, Prague.

Identifying Opinion Holders and Targets with Dependency Parser in Chinese News Texts

Bin Lu
Department of Chinese, Translation and Linguistics &
Language Information Sciences Research Centre
City University of Hong Kong
Kowloon, Hong Kong
lubin2010@gmail.com

Abstract

In this paper, we propose to identify opinion holders and targets with dependency parser in Chinese news texts, i.e. to identify opinion holders by means of reporting verbs and to identify opinion targets by considering both opinion holders and opinion-bearing words. The experiments with NTCIR-7 MOAT's Chinese test data show that our approach provides better performance than the baselines and most systems reported at NTCIR-7.

1 Introduction

In recent years, *sentiment analysis*, which mines opinions from information sources such as news, blogs and product reviews, has drawn much attention in the NLP field (Hatzivassiloglou and McKeown, 1997; Pang et al., 2002; Turney, 2002; Hu and Liu, 2004).

An opinion expressed in a text involves different components, including opinion expression, opinion holder and target (Wilson and Wiebe, 2003). Opinion holder is usually an entity that holds an opinion, and opinion target is what the opinion is about (Kim and Hovy, 2006). Although there have been research on identifying opinion holders and targets in English product reviews and news texts, little work has been reported on similar tasks involving Chinese news texts.

In this study, we investigate how dependency parsing can be used to help the task on opinion holder/target identification in Chinese news texts. Three possible contributions from this study are: 1) we propose that the existence of reporting verbs is a very important feature for identifying opinion holders in news texts, which has not been clearly indicated; 2) we argue that the identification of opinion targets should not be done alone without considering opinion holders, because opinion holders are much easier to be identified in news texts and the identified holders are quite useful for the identification of the associated targets. Our approach shows encouraging performance on opinion holder/target identification, and the results are much better than the baseline results and most results reported in NTCIR-7 (Seki et al., 2008).

The paper is organized as follows. Sec. 2 introduces related work. Sec. 3 gives the linguistic analysis of opinion holder/target. The proposed approach is described in Sec. 4, followed by the experiments in Sec. 5. Lastly we conclude in Sec. 6.

2 Related Work

Although document-level sentiment analysis (Turney, 2002; Pang et al., 2002) can provide the overall polarity of the whole text, it fails to detect the holders and targets of the sentiment in texts.

2.1 Opinion Holders/ Target Identification

For opinion mining of product reviews, opinion holder identification is usually omitted under the assumption that opinion holder is the review writer; and opinion targets are limited to the product discussed and its features (Hu and Liu, 2004). But in news texts, opinion holders/targets are more diverse: all named entities and noun phrases can be opinion holders; while opinion targets could be noun phrases, verb phrases or even clauses (Kim and Hovy, 2006; Ruppenhofer et al. 2008).

Bethard et al. (2004) identify opinion propositions and their holders by semantic parsing techniques. Choi et al. (2005) and Kim and Hovy (2005) identify only opinion holders on the MPQA corpus (Wilson and Wiebe, 2003). Kim and Hovy (2006) proposed to map the semantic frames of FrameNet into opinion holder and target for only adjectives and verbs. Kim et al. (2008) proposed to

Proceedings of the NAACL HLT 2010 Student Research Workshop, pages 46–51,
Los Angeles, California, June 2010.

use syntactic structures for target identification without considering opinion holders. Stoyanov and Cardie (2008) define opinion *topic* and *target* and treat the task as a co-reference resolution problem.

For the identification of opinion holders/targets in Chinese, there were several reports at NTCIR-7 (Seki et al., 2008). Xu et al. (2008) proposed to use some heuristic rules for opinion holder/target identification. Ku et al. (2008) treated opinion holder identification as a binary classification problem of determining if a word was a part of an opinion holder.

2.2 Chinese Dependency Parsing

Dependency structures represent all sentence relationships uniformly as typed dependency relations between pairs of words. Some major dependency relations for Chinese (Ma et al., 2004) include 主谓 (Subject-Verb, SBV), 动宾 (Verb-Object, VOB), 定中(Attributive-Noun, ATT), 数量 (Quantifier, QUN) and 独立结构(Independent structure, IS). Consider the following Chinese sentence:

a) 俄國 外長 伊凡諾夫 說，北約 東向 擴張是 " 邁向 錯誤的方向 " 。

Russian Foreign Minister Ivanov said that NATO's eastward expansion was "Towards the wrong direction."

Its dependency tree is shown in Figure1. Its head is the verb 說 (said), whose subject and object are respectively *俄国外长伊凡诺夫* (Russian Foreign Minister Ivanov) and the embedded clause *北約東向擴張是"邁向錯誤的方向"* (NATO's eastward expansion was "towards the wrong direction.").

3 Linguistic Analysis of Opinions

The opinions in news text may be explicitly mentioned or be expressed indirectly by the types of words and the style of language (Wilson and Wiebe, 2003). Two kinds of lexical clues are exploited here for opinion holder/target identification:

Reporting verbs: verbs indicating speech events;

Opinion-bearing Words: words or phrases containing polarity (i.e. positive, negative or neutral).

In sentence a) above, the reporting verb *說 (said)* indicates a speech event expressing an opinion given by the holder *俄国 外长 伊凡诺夫 (Russian Foreign Minister Ivanov)*. Meanwhile, the opinion-bearing word *錯誤 (wrong)* shows negative attitude towards the target *北約東向擴張 (NATO's eastward expansion)*.

Therefore, we assume that a large proportion of holders are governed by such reporting verbs, while targets are usually governed by opinion-bearing words/phrases.

Opinion holders are usually named entities, including, but not limited to, person names (e.g. 經濟學家歐爾/economist Ol), organization names (e.g. 英國政府/UK government), and personal titles (e.g. 經濟學家/the economist). Opinion holders can also be *common noun phrases*, such as 廠商 (companies), 兩千名學生 (two thousand students). *Pronouns*[1] can also be opinion holders, e.g. 他 (he), 他們 (they), 我(I). Opinion targets are more abstract and diverse, and could be agents, concrete objects, actions, events or even abstract ideas. In addition to noun phrases, opinion targets could also be *verb phrases* or *embedded clauses*.

4 Identifying Opinion Holders/Targets

In this section, we introduce our approach of identifying opinion holders/targets. We use the dependency parser in the HIT LTP package (http://ir.hit.edu.cn/) to get the dependency relations of the simplified Chinese sentences converted from the traditional Chinese ones.

4.1 Lexical Resources

The reporting verbs were firstly collected from the Chinese sample data of NTCIR-6 OAPT (Seki et al., 2007) in which the *OPINION_OPR* tag was used to mark them. We then use HowNet, WordNet and Tongyici Cilin to extend the reporting verbs from 68 to 308 words through manual synonym search. Some frequently used reporting verbs include 說(say), 表示(express), 認爲(think), etc. Some of the reporting verbs could also convey opinions, such as 批評 (criticize), 譴責 (condemn), 讚揚 (praise), etc.

For opinion-bearing words/phrases, we use *The Lexicon of Chinese Positive Words* (Shi and Zhu, 2006) and *The Lexicon of Chinese Negative Words* (Yang and Zhu, 2006), which consist of 5046 positive items and 3499 negative ones, respectively.

[1] The resolution of the anaphor or co-reference has not been dealt with yet, i.e. the identified holders of the sentence are assumed to be in the same form as it appears in the sentence.

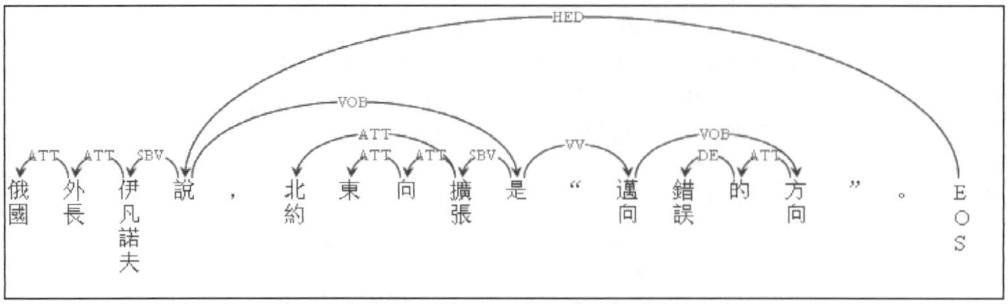

Figure 1. Dependency Tree for Sentence a)

4.2 Chinese Sentence Preprocessing (SP)

To enhance the robustness of the dependency parser, named entities are first recognized with a traditional Chinese word segmentation tool with access to the very large LIVAC dictionary (http://www.livac.org) collected from Chinese news published in Hong Kong and Taiwan. The identified named entities, as well as the collected reporting verbs and opinion-bearing words are added to the user dictionary of the HIT LTP package to help parsing.

Before parsing, the parentheses enclosing only English words or numbers are removed in sentences, because the parser cannot properly process the parentheses which may greatly influence the parsing result.

4.3 Identifying Opinion Holders with Reporting Verbs

4.3.1 Holder Candidate Generation

Two hypotheses are used to identify opinion holders in opinionated sentences: 1) the subject of reporting verbs will be the opinion holders; 2) if no reporting verb is found, the author could be the opinion holder. In addition to the two hypotheses above, the following heuristic rules (**HR**) are used:

1) Other words having relations with reporting verbs

If the subject of reporting verbs is not found in the sentence, we will find the word having relationship of *ATT*, *VOB* or *IS* with the reporting verbs, because sometimes the parser may wrongly marked the subject as other relations.

2) Colon processing in Headlines

If no reporting verbs are found in news headlines, we just pick up the noun before the colon as the target candidate in the headlines because the author usually replaces the reporting verb with a colon due to length limitation. E.g. in the headline *摩根*：經濟成長熄火 (*Morgan: Economic growth has been shut down*), the noun *摩根 (Morgan)* before colon is chosen as the opinion holder.

3) Holder in the previous sentence

If no opinion holder is found in the current clause and one holder candidate is found in the previous clause, we just choose the opinion holder of the previous clause as the holder candidate, because an opinion holder may express several ideas through consecutive sentences or clauses.

4.3.2 Holder Candidate Expansion (EP)

Through the procedure of candidate generation, we may find a holder candidate containing only one single word. But the holder may be a word sequence instead of a single word. Thus we further expand the holder candidates from the core head word by the following rules:

1) Attributive modifier (ATT)

E.g. in sentence a) mentioned in Sec. 2.2, the subject of the reporting verb *說 (said)* is *伊凡諾夫 (Ivanov)*, which has the attributive noun *外長 (Foreign Minister)* modified further by an attributive noun 俄國*(Russia)*. Therefore, the final extended opinion holder would be *外長伊凡諾夫 (Russian Foreign Minister Ivanov)*.

2) Quantifier modifier and 和/及 (and/or)

E.g. the quantifier modifier *部分(some)* in the noun phrase 部分亞洲國家 (some Asian countries) should be part of the opinion holder. Sometime, we need to extend the holder across *和/及(and/or)*, e.g. *蘇哈托和另外兩名軍方將領 (Suharto and two other army generals)*.

Furthermore, time nouns, numbers and words only containing one Chinese character (except for pronouns) are removed from the candidates, as they are unlikely to be opinion holders.

4.4 Identifying Opinion Targets with Opinion-bearing Words

Here we propose to use automatically identified reporting verbs and opinion holders to help opinion target identification. The heuristic rules (**HR**) are as follows.

1) If a candidate of opinion holder is automatically identified with a reporting verb in an opinionated sentence, we will try to find the subject in the embedded clause as the target candidate by the following two steps: a) Find the subject of the object verb of the reporting verb. E.g. in sentence a) in Sec. 2.2, the opinion target *北約東向擴張 (NATO's eastward expansion)* is the subject of the verb *是 (was)* in the embedded clause which is in turn the object of the reporting verb *說 (said)*; b) If no target candidate is found in step a, we try to find after the reporting verb the subject whose parent is an opinion-bearing word as the target candidate.

2) If no target candidate is found in step 1, and no opinion holder is found in the sentence, we find the subject of the sentence as the target candidate, because the author may be the opinion holder and the target could be the subject of the sentence.

3) If still no target candidate is found in step 2, we find the object in the sentence as the target because the object could be the opinion target in case there is no subject and no opinion holder.

Target candidate expansion (**EP**) is similar to holder candidate expansion described in Sec. 4.3.2. If an opinion target is in the opinion holder candidates (we call it *holder conflict*, **HC**), we remove it from the target candidates, and then try to find another using the above procedure.

5 Experiments

We use the traditional Chinese test data in NTCIR-7 MOAT (Seki et al., 2008) for our experiments. Out of 4465 sentences, 2174 are annotated as opinionated by the lenient standard, and the opinion holders of some opinionated sentences are marked as POST_AUTHOR denoting the author of the news article. We use the final list given by the organizers as the gold standard.

Baselines for opinion holder identification:

Baseline 1: We just use the subject of reporting verbs as the opinion holder, without sentence preprocessing described in Sec. 4.2 and any heuristic rules introduced in Sec. 4.3.1.

Baseline 2: We also implement the CRF model for detecting opinion holders (Choi et al., 2006) by using CRF++. The training data is the NTCIR-6 Chinese test data. The labels used by CRF comprise Holder, Parent of Holder, None (not holder or parent) and the features for each word in our implementation include: basic features (i.e. word, POS-tag, whether the word itself is a reporting verb or not), dependency features (i.e. parent word, POS-tag of its parent, dependency relation with its parent, whether its parent is a reporting verb) and semantic features (i.e. WSD entry in Tongyici Cilin, WSD entry of its parent).

Baseline for opinion target identification:

Baseline 1: we try to find the subject or object of opinion-bearing words as the targets. If both a subject and an object are found, we just simply choose the subject as the target.

We evaluate performance using 3 measures: exact match (EM), head match (HM), and partial match (PM), similar to Choi et al. (2006). We use three evaluation metrics: recall (Rec), precision (Pre), and F1. For opinion holder identification, we consider two cases: 1) all opinionated sentences; 2) only the opinionated sentences whose opinion holders do not contain *POST_AUTHOR*. The metric *ALL_Pre* reported below is the precision in case 1 which is the same with recall and F1.

5.1 Results for Opinion Holder Identification

The results for holder identification are shown in Table 1, from which we can observe that our proposed approach significantly outperforms the two baseline methods, including the unsupervised baseline 1 and the supervised baseline 2.

		ALL_Pre	Pre	Rec	F1
Baseline1	EM	52.4	46.8	31.6	37.8
	HM	67.1	80.2	54.2	64.7
	PM	72.1	**89.3**	60.4	72.0
Baseline2 (CRF)	EM	45.5	34.7	18.1	23.8
	HM	55.2	63.6	33.1	43.6
	PM	55.6	64.9	33.8	44.4
Our Approach	EM	**69.8**	**74.4**	**63.6**	**68.5**
	HM	**72.5**	**79.2**	**67.7**	**73.0**
	PM	**75.7**	85.1	**72.7**	**78.4**

Table 1. Results for Opinion Holders

Unexpectedly, even the unsupervised baseline 1 achieves better performance than baseline 2 (the CRF-based method). The possible reasons are: 1) the training data is not large enough to cover the cases in the test data, resulting in low recall of the CRF model; 2) the features used by the CRF model could be refined to improve the performance.

Here we also evaluate the influences of the following three factors on the performance: sentences preprocessing (SP) in Sec. 4.2, holder expansion (EP) in Sec. 4.3.2 and the heuristic rules (HR) in Sec. 4.3.1. The results are shown in Figure 2 for different combinations, in which BL refers to baseline 1.

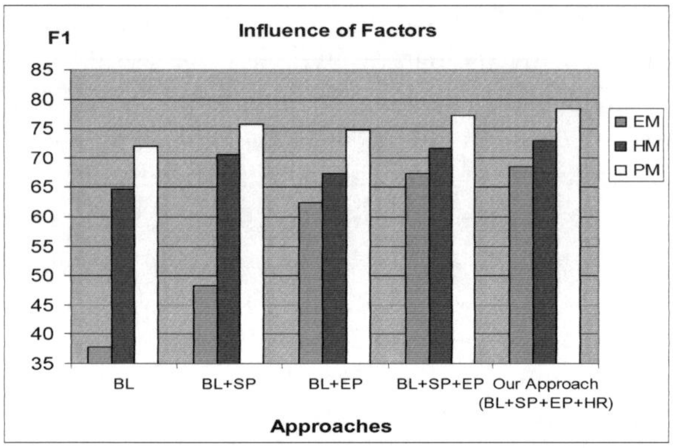

Figure 2. Influences of Factors on Opinion Holders

From Figure 2, we can observe that: 1) All three factors have positive effects on performance compared to baseline 1, and our approach by integrating all factors achieves the best performance; 2) SP improve the performance in terms of all three metrics, showing that SP including named entity recognition and parenthesis removing are useful for holder identification; 3) The major improvement of EP lies in EM, showing that the main contribution of EP is to get the exact opinion holders by expanding the core head noun; 4) SP+EP+HR improves the performance in terms of all three metrics compared with SP+HR, showing the heuristic rules are useful to improve the performance.

5.2 Results for Opinion Target Identification

The results for opinion target identification are shown in Table 2, from which we can observe that our proposed approach significantly outperforms the baseline method.

		Pre	Rec	F1
Baseline 1	EM	11.1	9.2	10.1
	HM	24.0	19.9	21.8
	PM	39.4	32.7	35.8
Our Approach	EM	**29.3**	**28.5**	**28.9**
	HM	**38.4**	**38.0**	**38.2**
	PM	**59.3**	**58.7**	**59.0**

Table 2. Results for Opinion Targets

We also investigate the influences of the following four factors on the performance: sentence preprocessing (SP) in Sec. 4.2, target expansion (EP) in Sec. 4.4, holder conflict (HC), the heuristic rules (HR) proposed in Sec. 4.4. The F1s for EM, HM and PM are shown in Figure 3, in which BL refers to baseline 1.

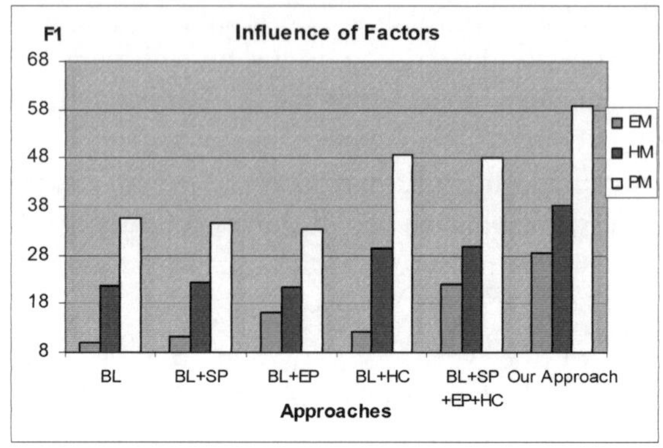

Figure 3. Influences of Factors on Opinion Targets

From Figure 3, we can observe that: 1) All four factors have positive effects on performance compared to the baseline, and our approach integrating all the factors achieves the best performance; 2) EP significantly improves F1 of EM without much improvement on F1 of HM or PM, showing that EP's major contribution lies in exact match; 3) The major contribution of HC is the improvement of F1s of HM and PM, showing the automatically identified opinion holders are quite helpful for finding opinion targets; 4) SP+EP+HC improves the performance in terms of all three metrics; and our approach further improves the performance by adding HR.

5.3 Discussion

Here we compare our results with those reported at NTCIR-7 MOAT traditional Chinese test (Seki et al., 2008). Without considering the errors in the previous step, the highest F1s for opinion holder analysis reported by the four participants were respectively 82.5%, 59.9%, 50.3% and 59.5%, and the highest F1s for target reported by the three participants were respectively 60.6%, 2.1% and 3.6%. Compared to the results at NTCIR-7, our performances on both opinion holder identification in Table 1 and that on target identification in Table 2 seem quite encouraging even by the EM metrics.

Consider the evaluation for opinion holders/targets was semi-automatic at NTCIR-7. We should note that although the generated standard had been supplemented by the participants' submissions, some correct answers may still be missing, especially for targets since only three teams participated in the target identification task and the recalls were not high. Thus the performance reported in Table 1 and 2 may be underestimated.

Here we also give an estimate on the percentages of opinionated sentences containing both opinion holders and at least one reporting verb in NTCIR-6 and NTCIR-7's traditional Chinese test data, which are respectively 94.5% and 83.9%. The high percentages show that reporting verbs are very common in news report.

6 Conclusion and Future Work

In this paper, we investigate the problem of identifying opinion holders/targets in opinionated sentences of Chinese news texts based on Chinese dependency parser, reporting verbs and opinion-bearing words. Our proposed approach shows encouraging performance on opinion holder/target identification with the NTCIR-7's traditional Chinese test data, and outperforms most systems reported at NTCIR-7 and the baseline methods including the CRF-based model.

The proposed approach is highly dependent on dependency parser, and we would like to further investigate machine learning approaches (including the CRF model) by treating dependency structures as one of the linguistic features, which could be more robust to parsing errors. Opinion targets are more difficult to be identified than opinion holders, and deserve more attention in the NLP field, and we also would extend the targets to verb phrases and embedded clauses in addition to noun phrases. To explore the effectiveness of our approach with English data such as MPQA is another direction.

Acknowledgements

We acknowledge the help of our colleagues (Professor Benjamin K. Tsou and Mr. Jiang Tao).

Reference

Steven Bethard, Hong Yu, Ashley Thornton, Vasileios Hatzivassiloglou, and Dan Jurafsky. 2004. Automatic Extraction of Opinion Propositions and their Holders, *AAAI Spring Symposium on Exploring Attitude and Affect in Text: Theories and Applications*.

Yejin Choi, Claire Cardie, Ellen Riloff, and Siddharth Patwardhan. 2005. Identifying sources of opinions with conditional random fields and extraction patterns. In *Proc. of HLT/EMNLP-05*.

Vasileios Hatzivassiloglou and Kathleen McKeown. 1997. Predicting the Semantic Orientation of Adjectives. In *Proc. of ACL-97*. 174-181.

Minqing Hu and Bing Liu. 2004. Mining Opinion Features in Customer Reviews. In *Proc. of AAAI-04*.

Soo-Min Kim and Eduard Hovy. 2005. Identifying Opinion Holders for Question Answering in Opinion Texts, In *Proc. of AAAI-05 Workshop on Question Answering in Restricted Domains*. Pittsburgh, PA.

Soo-Min Kim and Eduard Hovy. 2006. Extracting opinions, opinion holders, and topics expressed in online news media text, *In Proc. of ACL Workshop on Sentiment and Subjectivity in Text*.

Youngho Kim, Seongchan Kim, and Sung-Hyon Myaeng. 2008. Extracting Topic-related Opinions and their Targets in NTCIR-7, *Proc. of NTCIR-7 Workshop*, Tokyo, Japan.

Lun-Wei Ku, I-Chien Liu, Chia-Ying Lee, Kuan-hua Chen and Hsin-Hsi Chen. 2008. Sentence-Level Opinion Analysis by CopeOpi in NTCIR-7. In *Proc. of NTCIR-7 Workshop*. Tokyo, Japan.

Jinshan Ma, Yu Zhang, Ting Liu and Sheng Li. 2004. A statistical dependency parser of Chinese under small training data. *IJCNLP-04 Workshop: Beyond shallow analyses - Formalisms and statistical modeling for deep analyses*.

Bo Pang, Lillian Lee, and Shivakumar Vaithyanathan. 2002. Thumbs up? Sentiment classification using machine learning techniques. In *Proc. of EMNLP-02*.

Josef Ruppenhofer, Swapna Somasundaran, Janyce Wiebe. 2008. Finding the Sources and Targets of Subjective Expressions. In *Proc. of LREC 2008*.

Yohei Seki, David Kirk Evans, Lun-Wei Ku, and et al. 2007. Overview of Opinion Analysis Pilot Task at NTCIR-6. *Proc. of the NTCIR-6 Workshop*.

Yohei Seki, David Kirk Evans, Lun-Wei Ku, and et al. 2008. Overview of Multilingual Opinion Analysis Task at NTCIR-7. *Proc. of the NTCIR-7 Workshop*. Japan. 2008. 12.

Jilin Shi and Yinggui Zhu. 2006. The Lexicon of Chinese Positive Words (褒義詞詞典). Sichuan Lexicon Press.

Veselin Stoyanov and Claire Cardie. 2008. Topic Identification for Fine-Grained Opinion Analysis. In *Proc. of COLING-08*.

Peter D. Turney. 2002. Thumbs up or thumbs down? Semantic orientation applied to unsupervised classification of reviews, In *Proc. of ACL-02*.

Theresa Wilson and Janyce Wiebe. 2003. Annotating opinions in the world press. *Proc. of the 4th ACL SIGdial Workshop on Discourse and Dialogue (SIGdial-03)*.

Ruifeng Xu, Kam-Fai Wong and Yunqing Xia. 2008. Coarse-Fine Opinion Mining - WIA in NTCIR-7 MOAT Task. *Proc. of the 7th NTCIR Workshop*.

Ling Yang and Yinggui Zhu. 2006. The Lexicon of Chinese Negative Words (貶義詞詞典). Sichuan Lexicon Press.

A Data Mining Approach to Learn Reorder Rules for SMT

Avinesh PVS
IIIT Hyderabad
Language Technologies Research Centre
avinesh@research.iiit.ac.in

Abstract

In this paper, we describe a syntax based source side reordering method for phrase-based statistical machine translation (SMT) systems. The source side training corpus is first parsed, then reordering rules are automatically learnt from source-side phrases and word alignments. Later the source side training and test corpus are reordered and given to the SMT system. Reordering is a common problem observed in language pairs of distant language origins. This paper describes an automated approach for learning reorder rules from a word-aligned parallel corpus using association rule mining. Reordered and generalized rules are the most significant in our approach. Our experiments were conducted on an English-Hindi EILMT corpus.

1 Introduction

In recent years SMT systems (Brown et al., 1990), (Yamada and Knight, 2001), (Chiang, 2005), (Charniak et al., 2003) have been in focus. It is easy to develop a MT system for a new pair of languages using an existing SMT system and a parallel corpora. It isn't a surprise to see SMT being attractive in terms of less human labour as compared to traditional rule-based systems. However to achieve good scores SMT requires large amounts of sentence aligned parallel text. Such resources are available only for few languages, whereas for many languages the online resources are low. So we propose an approach for a pair of resource rich and resource poor languages.

Some of the previous approaches include (Collins et al., 2005), (Xia and McCord, 2004). Former describes an approach for reordering the source sentence in German-English MT system. Their approach involves six transformations on the parsed source sentence. Later propose an approach which automatically extracts rewrite patterns by parsing the source and target sides of the training corpus for French-English pair. These rewritten patterns are applied to the source sentence so that the source and target word orders are similar. (Costa-jussà and Fonollosa, 2006) consider Part-Of-Speech (POS) based source reordering as a translation task. These approaches modify the source language word order before decoding in order to produce a word order similar to the target language. Later the reordered sentence is given as an input to the standard phrase-based decoder to be translated without the reordering condition.

We propose an approach along the same lines those described above. Here we follow a data mining approach to learn the reordering/rewrite rules applied on an English-Hindi MT system. The rest of the paper is organized as follows. In Section 2 we briefly describe our approach. In Section 3 we present a rule learning framework using Association Rule Mining (Agrawal et al., 1993). Section 4 consists of experimental setup and sample rules learnt. We present some discussion in Section 5 and finally detail proposed future work in Section 6.

Proceedings of the NAACL HLT 2010 Student Research Workshop, pages 52–57,
Los Angeles, California, June 2010.

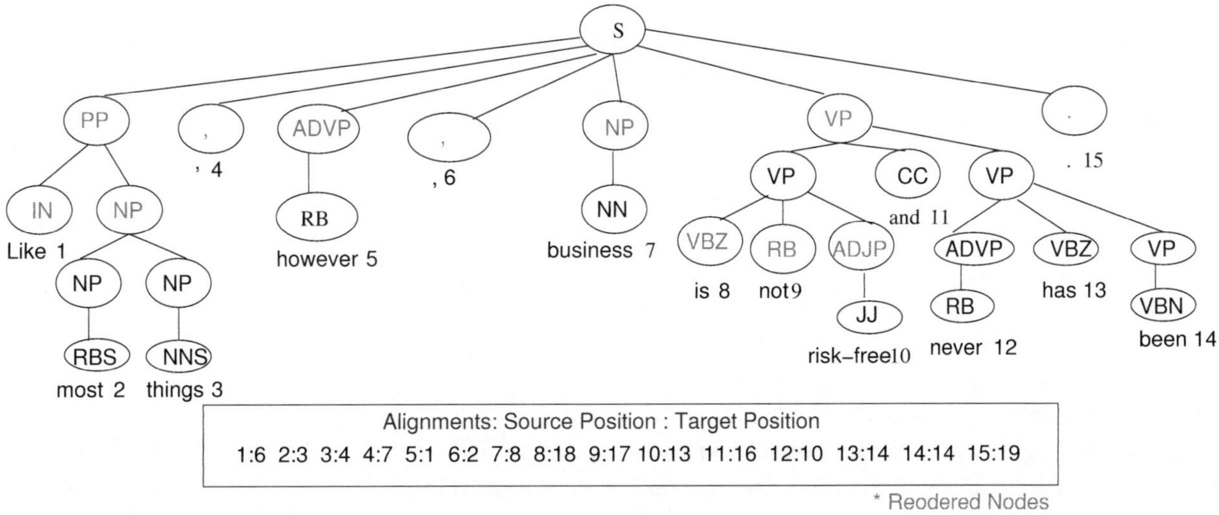

Figure 1: English-Hindi Example

2 Approach

Our approach is inspired by Association rule mining, a popular concept in data mining for discovering interesting relations between items in large transaction records. For example, the rule {milk, bread} ⇒ {butter} found in the customer database would indicate if a customer buys milk and bread together, he or she is also likely to buy butter. Similar notions can be projected to the learning of reorder rules. For example, {NNP, VB, NNP} ⇒ {1,3,2} would indicate if NNP,VB and NNP occur together in source text, then its ordering on the target side would be {1,3,2}. The original problem of association rule mining doesn't consider the order of items in the rule, whereas in our problem order is important as well.

In this approach we start with extracting the most frequent patterns from the English language model. The English language model consists of both POS and chunk tag n-gram model built using SRILM toolkit [1]. Then to learn the reordering rules for these patterns we used a word-aligned English-Hindi parallel corpus, where the alignments are generated using GIZA++ (Och and Ney, 2003). These alignments are used to learn the rewrite rules by calculating the target positions of the source nodes. Fig 1 shows an English phrase structure tree (PS) [2] and its alignments corresponding to the target sentence.

2.1 Calculation of target position:

Target position of a node is equal to the target position of the **head** among the children (Aho and Ullman, 1972). For example the head node of a NP is the right most NN, NNP, NNS (or) NNX. Rules developed by Collins are used to calculate the head node (Collins, 2003).

Psn(T,Node)=Psn(T,Head(Node))

In Fig 1, Position of VP in target side is 18.

Psn(T,VP)=Psn(T,Head(VP))=Psn(T,VBZ)=18

3 Association rule mining

We modified the original definition by Rakesh Agarwal to suit our needs (Agrawal et al., 1993; Srikant and Agrawal, 1995) . The problem here is defined as: Let $E=P:\{e_1,e_2,e_3,...e_n\}$ be a sequence of N children of a node P. Let $A=\{a_1,a_2,a_3,...a_n\}$ be the alignment set of the corresponding set E.

Let $D=P:\{S_1,S_2,S_3,...S_m\}$ be set consisting of all possible ordered sequence of children of the node P, Ex: S_1=S:{NP,VP,NP}, where S is the parent node and NP, VP and NP are its children. Each set in D has a unique ID, which represents the occurrence of the source order of the children. A rule is defined as an implication of the form $X \Rightarrow Y$ where $X \subseteq E$ and

[1] http://www-speech.sri.com/projects/srilm/

[2] Stanford Parser: http://nlp.stanford.edu/software/lex-parser.shtml

Y⊆Target Positions(E,A). The sets of items X and Y are called LHS and RHS of the rule. To illustrate the concepts, we use a simple example from the English-Hindi parallel corpus.

Consider the set of items I={Set of POS tags} ⋃ {Set of Chunk tags}. For Example, I={NN,VBZ,NNS,NP,VP} and an example rule could be {NN,VBZ,NNS} ⇒ {1,3,2}, which means that when NN, VBZ and NNS occur in a continuous pattern they are reordered to 1,3 and 2 positions respectively on the target side. The above example is a naive example. If we consider the training corpus with the alignments we could use constraints on various measures of significance. We use the best-known constraints, namely minimum threshold support and confidence. The support supp(X) of an itemset X is defined as the proportion of sentences which contain the itemset. The confidence of a rule is defined as

$$conf(X \Rightarrow Y)=supp(X \bigcup Y)/supp(X).$$

Association rules require language specific minimum support and minimum confidence at the same time. To achieve this, association rule learning is done in two steps. Firstly, minimum support is applied to find all frequent itemsets in the source language model. In the second step, these frequent itemsets and the minimum confidence constraints are used to generate rules from the word-aligned parallel corpus.

3.1 Frequent Pattern mining

For the first task of collecting the most frequent itemsets we used Fpgrowth algorithm [3] (Borgelt, 2005) implemented by Christian Borgelt. We used a POS and a chunk tag English language model. In a given parse tree the pattern model based on the order of pre-terminals is called POS language model and the pattern model based on the Non-terminals is called the Chunk language model. The below algorithm is run on every Non-terminal and pre-terminal node of a parse tree. In the modified version of mining frequent itemsets we also include generalization of the frequent sets, similar to the work done by (Chiang, 2005).

Steps for extracting frequent LHSs: Consider $X_1,X_2,X_3,X_4,...X_x$ are all possible children of a node S. The transaction here is the sequence of children of the node S. The sample example is shown in Fig 2.

1. Collect all occurrences of the children of a node and their frequencies from the transactions and name the set L_1.

2. Calculate $L_2=L_1 * L_1$ which is the frequency set of two elements.

3. Similarly calculate L_n, till n = maximum possible children of parent S.

4. Once the maximum possible set is calculated, K-best frequent sets are collected and then elements which occur above a threshold(Θ) are combined to form a single element.
   Ex, most common patterns occurring as a children of NP are {JJ,NN,NN},{JJ,NN} etc.

5. The threshold was calculated based on various experiments, and then set to Θ=20% less than the frequency of least frequent itemset between the elements of the two L's.

   For example,
   L_3={JJ,NN}*{NN}={JJ,NN,NNP}.
   If freq{JJ,NN}=10, and freq{NNP}=20 and {JJ,NN,NNP}=9, Θ=10-(20% of 10)=8.
   So {JJ,NN} ⇒ X_1.

   This way the generalized rules are learnt for all the tables (L_n, L_{n-1}..L_3). Using these generalized rules, the initial transactions are modified.

6. Recalculate $L_1,L_2,..L_n$ based on the rules learnt above. Continue the process until no new rules are extracted at the end of the iteration.

3.2 Generate rules

The second problem is to generate association rules for these large itemsets with the constraints of minimal confidence. Suppose one of the large itemsets of a parent node S is L_k, L_k = P:{$e_1,e_2,,e_k$ }, association rules with these itemsets are generated in the following way: Firstly a set P:{ $e_1,e_2,..e_k$ } is

[3] http://www.borgelt.net/fpgrowth.html

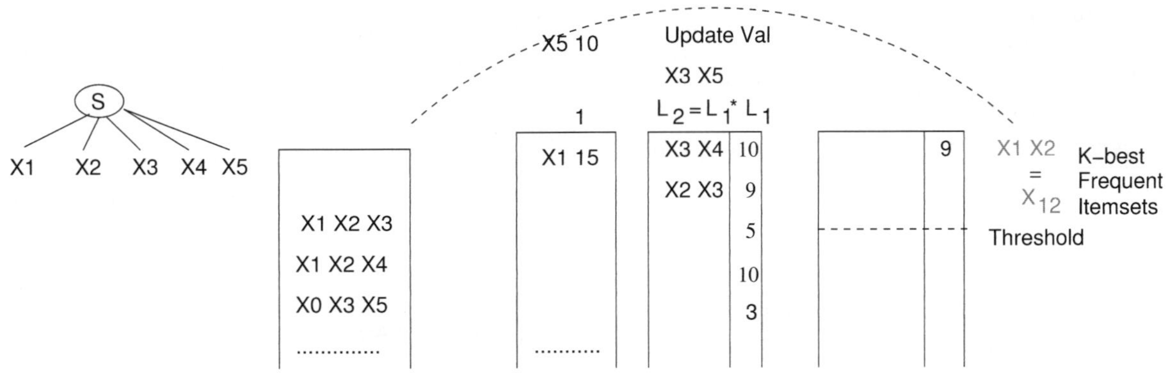

Figure 2: N-stage Generalization

matched with the source sequences of parent P and then their corresponding alignment information is used to generate the target sequence. The numbers on the rhs represent the position of the elements in the target sentence. Then by checking the constraint confidence this rule can be determined as interesting or not. Constraint confidence used here is the probability of occurrence of the non-monotone rule.

If $c_1, c_2, c_3, c_4 ... c_x$ are the children of a Node X. LHS is the original order of the children. RHS is the sorted order of the children on the basis of $Psn(T,Psn(S,c_i))$, where $1 \leq i \leq x$.

From Fig 1, let us consider the top node and find the rule based on the head based method.

Suppose that given from the above frequency rule

L_k = S:{'PP' ',' 'ADVP' ',' 'NP' 'VP'}

Children(S) = 'PP' ',' 'ADVP' ',' 'NP' 'VP' '.'

The target positions are calculated as shown in the Table 1. RHS is calculated based on the target positions.

Table 1: Target Positions of Children(S)

Psn(T,'PP')	= Psn(T,1)	=6
Psn(T,',')	= Psn(T,4)	=7
Psn(T,'ADVP')	= Psn(T,5)	=1
Psn(T,',')	= Psn(T,6)	=2
Psn(T,'NP')	=Psn(T,7)	=8
Psn(T,'VP')	=Psn(T,8)	=18
Psn(T,'.')	= Psn(T,15)	=19

LHS = PP , ADVP , NP VP .
RHS = 3 4 1 2 5 6 7

3.2.1 Use of Generalization:

The above rule generated is the most commonly occurring phenomenon in English to Hindi machine translation. It is observed that adverbial phrase generally occurs at the beginning of the sentence on the Hindi side. The rule generated above will be captured less frequently because the exact pattern in LHS is rarely matched. Using the above generalization in frequent itemset mining we can merge all the most frequent occurring patterns into a common pattern.

The above example pattern is modified to the below using the generalization technique.

Rule: X1 ADVP , X2 ⇒ 2 3 1 4

3.2.2 Rules and their Application

These generated rules are taken to calculate the probability of the non-monotone rules with respect to monotone rules. If the probability of the non-monotone rule was ≥ 0.5 then the rule was appended to the final list. The final list included all the generalized and non-generalized rules of different parent nodes.

The final list of rules is applied on both training and test corpus based on the longest possible sequence match. If the rule matches, then the source structures are reordered as per the rule. Specific rules are given more priority over the generalized rules.

4 Experiments

Table 2, Table 3 show some of the high frequency and generalized rules. The total number of rules learnt were 727 for a 11k training corpus. Number of generalizations learnt were 54.

Table 2: Most Frequent Rules

Rule	LHS	RHS
1	IN NP	2 1
2	NP VP NP	1 3 2
3	NP PP	2 1
4	VBG PP	2 1
5	VBZ ADVP NP	2 3 1

Table 3: Generalized Rules

Rule	LHS	RHS
1	X_1 ADVP , X_2	2 3 1 4
2	X_3 VBZ‖VBG X_4	1 3 2
3	ADVP X_5 .	2 1 3
4	MD RB X_6	3 1 2
5	VB X_7 NP-TMP	2 3 1

Once the training and test sentences are reordered using the above rules, they are fed to the Moses system. It is clear that without reordering the performace of the system is worst. Training and test data consisted of 11,300 and 500 sentences respectively.

Table 4: Evaluation on Moses

Config	Blue Score	NIST
Moses Without Reorder	0.2123	5.5315
Moses + Our Reorder	0.2329	5.6605
Moses With Reorder	0.2475	5.7069

5 Discussion

Our method showed a drop in terms of blue score as compared to Moses reordering; this is probably due to the reordering based on lexicalized rules in Moses. The above generalization works effectively in case of the Stanford parser as it stitches the nodes at top level. English-Hindi tourism corpus distributed as a part of ICON 2008 shared task. Our learning based on phrase structure doesn't handle the movement of children across nodes. Whereas, dependency structure based rule learning would help in handling more constructs in terms of word-level reordering patterns. Some of the least frequent patterns are actually interesting patterns in terms of reordering. Learning these kinds of patterns would be a challenging task.

6 Future Work

Work has to be done in terms of prioritization of the rules, for example first priority should be given to more specific rules (the one with constraints) then to the general rules. More constraints with respect to morphological features would also help in improving the diversity of the rules. We will also look into the linguistic clause based reordering features which would help in reordering of distant pair of languages. Manual evaluation of the output will throw some light on the effectiveness of this system. To further evaluate the approach we would also try the approach on someother distant language pairs.

References

Rakesh Agrawal, Tomasz Imieliński, and Arun Swami. 1993. Mining association rules between sets of items in large databases. In *SIGMOD '93: Proceedings of the 1993 ACM SIGMOD international conference on Management of data*, pages 207–216, New York, NY, USA. ACM.

Alfred V. Aho and Jeffrey D. Ullman. 1972. *The Theory of Parsing, Translation and Compiling*, volume 1. Prentice-Hall, Englewood Cliffs, NJ.

Christian Borgelt. 2005. An implementation of the fp-growth algorithm. In *OSDM '05: Proceedings of the 1st international workshop on open source data mining*, pages 1–5, New York, NY, USA. ACM.

Peter F. Brown, John Cocke, Stephen A. Della Pietra, Vincent J. Della Pietra, Fredrick Jelinek, John D. Lafferty, Robert L. Mercer, and Paul S. Roossin. 1990. A statistical approach to machine translation. *COMPUTATIONAL LINGUISTICS*, 16(2):79–85.

Eugene Charniak, Kevin Knight, and Kenji Yamada. 2003. Syntax-based language models for statistical machine translation. In *MT Summit IX. Intl. Assoc. for Machine Translation*.

David Chiang. 2005. A hierarchical phrase-based model for statistical machine translation. In *In ACL*, pages 263–270.

Michael Collins, Philipp Koehn, and Ivona Kučerová. 2005. Clause restructuring for statistical machine translation. In *ACL '05: Proceedings of the 43rd Annual Meeting on Association for Computational Linguistics*, pages 531–540, Morristown, NJ, USA. Association for Computational Linguistics.

Michael Collins. 2003. Head-driven statistical models for natural language parsing. Technical report.

Marta R. Costa-jussà and José A. R. Fonollosa. 2006. Statistical machine reordering. In *EMNLP '06: Proceedings of the 2006 Conference on Empirical Methods in Natural Language Processing*, pages 70–76, Morristown, NJ, USA. Association for Computational Linguistics.

Franz Josef Och and Hermann Ney. 2003. A systematic comparison of various statistical alignment models. *Computational Linguistics*, 29(1):19–51.

Ramakrishnan Srikant and Rakesh Agrawal. 1995. Mining generalized association rules. In *Research Report RJ 9963, IBM Almaden Research.*

Fei Xia and Michael McCord. 2004. Improving a statistical mt system with automatically learned rewrite patterns. In *COLING '04: Proceedings of the 20th international conference on Computational Linguistics*, page 508, Morristown, NJ, USA. Association for Computational Linguistics.

Kenji Yamada and Kevin Knight. 2001. A syntax-based statistical translation model. In *ACL '01: Proceedings of the 39th Annual Meeting on Association for Computational Linguistics*, pages 523–530, Morristown, NJ, USA. Association for Computational Linguistics.

Fine-Tuning in Brazilian Portuguese-English Statistical Transfer Machine Translation: Verbal Tenses

Lucia Silva
University of São Paulo
Av. Prof. Luciano Gualberto, 403
Cidade Universitária, São Paulo, BR
helena.rozario@usp.br

Abstract

This paper describes an experiment designed to evaluate the development of a Statistical Transfer-based Brazilian Portuguese to English Machine Translation system. We compare the performance of the system with the inclusion of new syntactic written rules concerning verbal tense between the Brazilian Portuguese and English languages. Results indicate that the system performance improved compared with an initial version of the system. However significant adjustments remain to be done.

1 Introduction

Recently, Statistical Machine Translation systems have received much attention because they are fully automated and have shown significant improvements over other types of approaches. Experiments with string-to-string and syntax-based systems have shown better results when linguistic features are added to Machine Translation systems (Chiang et al., 2009). The Statistical Transfer (Stat-XFER) approach presented in this paper was designed as a Statistical approach with a grammar module, which encodes syntactic transfer rules, i.e., rules which encode constituent structures from the source language to the target language structure.

Verbal tenses vary among natural languages. Each language has its typical verbal form, and they share mood, voice, aspect and person qualities (Comrie, 1993). Some languages, such as Portuguese and English do not share the same properties and the number of verbal tenses may present divergences. Our goal is to test the development of the Statistical Transfer-based system under the application of syntactic transfer rules of verbal tenses involving this pair of languages.

2 The Statistical Transfer-based system

The hybrid Stat-XFER system uses a transfer-based method and statistical paradigm for the translation process and it is composed of the following main components: the Bilingual Phrasal Lexicon, Morphology, Transfer Engine and the Decoder. Given one sentence in the source language, this input will go through all those components until the system outputs a set of pairs mapping candidate translations to probabilities. The Stat-XFER framework is shown in the figure 1 below.

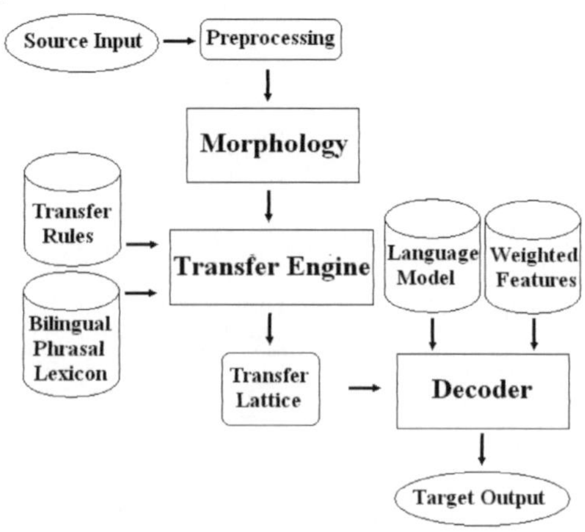

Figure 1. The Stat-XFER framework

Proceedings of the NAACL HLT 2010 Student Research Workshop, pages 58–63,
Los Angeles, California, June 2010.

Bilingual Phrasal Lexicon. The Portuguese-English lexicon is made up of a word-level lexicon. The lexicon was automatically extracted from the EUROPARL corpus[1] and in order to adjust it to this system's needs, this lexicon has been modified with new entries and deleted of the repeated entries.

Morphology. The system uses the Jspell[2] morphology analyzer, which was developed by the Minho University in Portugal. Jspell produces all possible labels for a lexical entry in the input and it provides a stem for each word with a different label. Upon each sentence in the lexicon input, the Morphology Analyzer examines each lexical entry and performs its analysis.

Transfer Engine. This component was developed by the AVENUE group from Carnegie Mellon University (Probst et al., 2002, Lavie et al., 2003, Lavie et al., 2004, Lavie 2008) and applies the lexical transfer rules specified by the Lexicon component, i.e. the lexical entries in Portuguese are substituted by their translations in English. This component also applies the transfer grammar rules from Portuguese into English producing constituents translated into the English structure. When the transfer stage has completed, we have a chart (hypergraph) in which each key contains an n-best beam for each non-terminal type of each source span. Each entry in the beam has a unification feature structure and log-linear feature scores associated with it.

Before decoding, the chart is turned into a lattice by removing hierarchical structure and respecting only the target-side ordering of the constituents produced by the grammar. The unification features and unification constraints on each rule can remove ungrammatical hypotheses from the search space.

Decoder. For each sentence, the Decoder does a monotonic left-to-right decoding on the Translation Lattice with no reordering beyond what the grammar produced. For each source span, the decoder keeps the *n* most likely hypotheses.

3 Experiment

According to Ma and McKeown (2009), in translations the main verb of a sentence is the most important element for the sentence comprehension. In Machine Translation, the goal is to produce understandable translations. Therefore, we started our experiment by adjusting the verbal tense rules between the Brazilian Portuguese and English.

Natural languages do not share the same properties concerning verbs. The pair of languages Portuguese and English for example, has different systems of modality. According to Palmer (1986), the English language has its system of modal verbs defined by *can*, *could*, *will*, *would*, *may*, *must*, *might*, *ought*, *shall*, *should*, *need* and *dare*. However, the Portuguese language has a system of mood consisting of *indicative* and *subjunctive* moods (Bechara, 2002).

Moreover, the Brazilian Portuguese and the English languages present morphological differences between verbal forms. For example, many verbs in English have the following form: Base + {-s form (3rd person singular present)/PAST/-ing/-ed} (Quirk and Greenbaum, 1973). Nonetheless, in Brazilian Portuguese the verbs present the following form in most case: Base + thematic vowel + number/person agreement + tense/mood agreement. This verbal form is present in every tense in the *indicative* and *subjunctive* moods.

In order not to lose any information concerning the distinction between verbal tenses from Brazilian Portuguese to English, we built a corpus with sentences in all verbal tenses in Portuguese (Bechara, 2002) and manually mapped them into English. Each Portuguese verbal form was mapped into English in all their conceivable translations. This corpus is a sentence-level parallel corpus with original sentences in the Portuguese language and their respective translations. The main goal of building this corpus was to verify all possible translations between Portuguese and English verbal tenses.

3.1 Methodology

Since this was a pilot experiment, we were interested in verifying if our changes improved the system. This pilot experiment consists of translating a corpus containing all three verb conjugation classes in Portuguese: 1) First conjugation class: verbs ending in –AR; 2) Second conjugation class:

[1] http://www.statmt.org/europarl/
[2] http://linguateca.di.uminho.pt/webjspell/jsolhelp.pl

verbs which end in –ER; and 3) Third Conjugation class: verbs ending in –IR, respecting each tense, mood and number in Stat-XFER system and then evaluating their results.

To construct the three corpora – one corpus for each conjugation class – we extracted the 100 most frequent Portuguese verbs appearing in Google's search engine[3] in all three conjugation classes in Portuguese. The search for the most frequent Portuguese verbs was done using a tool developed in Python and followed the following constrains: a) a result had to be an infinitive verb; b) had to be in the Portuguese language and c) had to be found in a Brazilian Web page.

From the one hundred most frequent Portuguese verbs in each conjugation class we manually built three corpora of all three verb conjugation classes in Portuguese, respecting each tense, mood, number, and person, and then a human translator mapped them into English through manual translation. Each corpus contains no more than three examples of each most frequent verb selected, resulting in 163 sentences.

Once all verbal tenses were translated into English, we applied these three corpora to the Stat-XFER system and evaluated all resulting translations using Meteor. Meteor is a metric for the evaluation of Machine Translation output. The metric is based on the harmonic mean of unigram precision and recall (Lavie and Agarwal, 2007). The Meteor scores are in a scale from 0 to 1, where 0 means the translation is the farthest from the reference translation and 1 means the translation is most similar to a human translation.

After the evaluation, we initiated the improvement of the grammar module with new syntactic transfer rules in order to deal with the problems presented by the differences between the verbal tenses. The transfer rules were manually developed and encoded how constituent structures in the source language transfer to the target language. In the beginning of our research, the system had 113 such rules in its grammar, but with some modifications the system now has 152 rules concerning the mapping from Portuguese to English. We add a rule for each tense in each conjugation class. Few rules address more than one tense. A Stat-XFER syntactic rule example is shown below.

```
1 {VP, 2}
2 ;;SL: ANDO
3 ;;TL: WALK
4 VP::VP [V] → [V]
5 (
6   (X1::Y1)
7   ((X1 tense) = c pres)
8   ((X1 mood) =c (*NOT* subj))
9   ((Y1 tense) = pres)
10  ((X0 number) = (X1 number))
11  ((X0 person) = (X1 person))
12 )
```

The first line is the name of rule, in this case *VP, 2*. The second and third lines are examples of transference between both languages, which means a source language (*SL*) will be encoded into a respective target language (*TL*). The forth line indicates that a simple verb in *SL* will be translated as a simple verb in *TL* as well.

The condition of application of that rules is between parenthesis, shown in the fifth and twelfth lines. In line six, inside these parentheses, it is indicated that the first element of the verbal phrase from source language, i.e. *X1*, will be converted as the first element of the verbal phrase in the target language, i.e. *Y1*. Line seven says that *X1* must be in the present tense and line eight says it must not be a subjunctive mood. Line nine states that *Y1* must be in the present tense. Lines ten and eleven indicate that *X1* will receive the number and person from an element in the source language, *X0* in this case.

Another significant modification concerns the Bilingual phrasal lexicon. In the beginning of our research, the system had 56.665 entries with their respective translations. However, many of these lexical items presented improper translations, repetitions and lack of correct meanings. To help improve the development of our system some modifications in this lexicon were required. This word level lexicon is in constant modification with the inclusion of missing lexicon items, cleaning of repeated items and correction of the inappropriate ones. The Stat-XFER word-level lexicon has now 57.315 entries with their respective translations.

3.2 Results

After the insertion of new syntactic rules, adjustment of the existing (old) rules and the modifica-

[3] http://www.google.com.br

tions in the lexicon, we translated the same three corpora again to evaluate the performance one more time. The comparative results of these two evaluations are shown in Table 1 and Figure 2 below.

Corpora	System in the initial state	System in the current state
1st conjugation class	0.5346	0.5184
2nd conjugation class	0.5182	0.5269
3rd conjugation class	0.5291	0.5356

Table 1. Meteor evaluation of initial and current state of the system

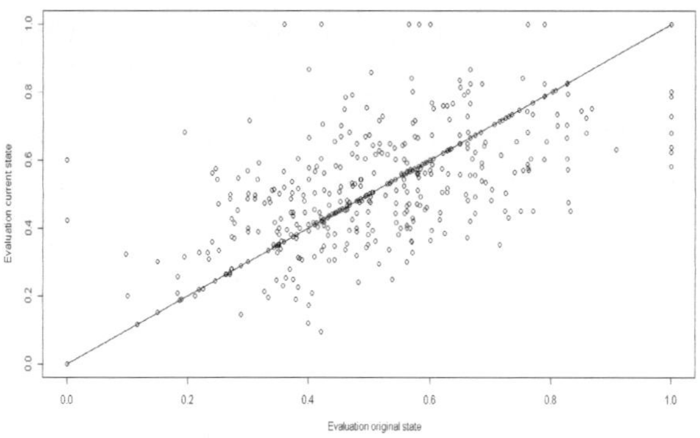

Figure 2.The graphic shows evaluation results of a sample of 489 sentences distributed across all verbal tense, mood, number and person in English during the initial stage and the current stage of the development of the Stat-XFER system. Results are in a scale of 0 to 1. 0 means the translation is the farthest from the reference translation and 1 means the translation is most correlated to a human translation. Each entry in the picture corresponds to one sentence evaluated according to the Meteor metric, distributed in the x-axis (initial evaluation) and the y-axis (current evaluation). The 45o line distinguishes those cases where performance of one evaluation was better than the other.

Interesting results were collected in this experiment. The new results show improvements in correlation with translation references on the second and third conjugations (Table 1). The system modifications we have done so far yielded some improvements. The inclusion and correction of syntactic rules according to the differences between linguistic parameters of the languages is the natural way to improve the results of Meteor evaluation in Stat-XFER system.

However, it is also noticeable that in the first conjugation we observed a decline in the performance of the system. This was one of the interesting observations we made based on this study.

To better study the effect of the inclusion of new grammar rules between verbal tenses, we perform a second evaluation of our system, now using a previously unseen corpus. This new corpus was build from FAPESP Magazine[4], which is a bilingual online publication designed for the Brazilian scientific community. We extracted 415 sentences from the Humanities section and translated them with the old and new syntactic rules to evaluate the performance of the system. The comparative results of these two evaluations are shown in Table 2 below.

FAPESP Corpus	System in the initial state	System in the current state
Humanities section	0.2884	0.5565

Table 2. Meteor evaluation of initial and actual state of the system

The two evaluations of the FAPESP Magazine corpus indicate that the insertion of new grammar rules presents significant improvement compared to the system in its initial state. It is important to note that these results validate our experiment and confirm the improvement of the system. We discuss our results in Section 4.

4 Discussion

An interesting observation is that in the corpus manually built for the experiment, the score of the first conjugation decreased (Table 1), while we expected that it should increase. We were surprised by this phenomenon and started investigating its causes. After preliminary studies, we now believe that this is due to a greater number of possible meanings that verbs from the first conjugation in Portuguese can assume, thus producing several translations in English, with smaller a correlation with respective human reference translations.

According to Williams (1962), the endings of infinitive verbs in Portuguese are derived from Classical Latin. The first conjugation in Brazilian Portuguese also contains verbs borrowed from dif-

[4] http://revistapesquisa.fapesp.br

ferent languages, e.g. the English verb *to delete* has its correspondent *deletar* in Portuguese. Moreover, the creation of new verbs in Portuguese is always included in the first conjugation, sharing a common set of characteristic of verbs ended in –AR. While the second and third conjugation classes tend to have a finite number of verbs given from Classical Latin, the first conjugation class is still increasing, unlike the second and third conjugations. These changes in verbs from the first conjugation classes may impact the development and evaluation of the system.

Note that the corpora used to evaluate our system are very small compared to corpora recommend for Machine Translation evaluations. Since this was a pilot experiment, we were only interested in verifying if the questions we wanted to ask were answerable. Further validation will be performed once more rules are added to the system and new human translations are included in the reference corpus.

Lavie et al. (2004) applied a transfer-rule learning approach to this system in order to learn automatically the transfer rules from Hebrew to English. We believe that this approach can be applied to the Portuguese-to-English system and it can improve the coverage of grammar rules.

5 Conclusion

The results of our experiment are very promising. We could observe a clear improvement in the performance of the system after syntactic rules were added to its grammar module. The new syntactic rules concerning the verbal tenses improved system performance, but also indicated that there is significant room for improvements in the Stat-XFER system. In particular, improving the transfer rules in other aspects beyond the Verbal tense is a promising area of future research.

Although this research is in a preliminary stage, we already made interesting linguistic observations about Portuguese verbs from first conjugation concerning the development of Machine Translation systems. We believe this is a general issue that should concern every designer of Machine Translation system of the Brazilian Portuguese language. We are very excited about the future stages of this study, and its potential contribution to the linguistic perspective of the field of Machine Translation.

Acknowledgments

We would like to thank Fidel Beraldi and Indaiá Bassani from University of São Paulo, for developing the Python tool, which extracts the frequency of the verbs from Google search engine; Bianca Oliveira from Primacy Translations for translating the corpus reference; Jonathan Clark from Carnegie Mellon University for helping the authors with clarifications about the system; Marcello Modesto from University of São Paulo, for advisorship and Alon Lavie from Carnegie Mellon University, for hospitality and technical clarifications. The author acknowledges that the initial Stat-XFER system was developed jointly by Modesto, Lavie and the entire AVENUE group (www.cs.cmu.edu/~avenue).

References

Chiang, D., Knight, K. and W. Wang. 2009. 11,001 New Features for Statistical Machine Translation. *Proceedings of NAACL-HLT.*

Comrie, B. 1993. Tense. Cambridge University Press.

Ma, W., McKeown, K. 2009. Where's the Verb? Correcting Machine Translation During Answering. *Proceedings of the ACL-IJCNLP.*

Bechara, E. 2002. *Moderna gramática do Português.* Lucerna.

Lavie, A., Vogel, S., Levin, L., Peterson, E., Probst, K., Font Llitjos, A., Reynolds, R., Carbonell, J., and Cohen, R. 2003. Experiments with a Hindi-to-English Transfer-based MT System under a Miserly Data Scenario. *ACM Transactions on Asian Language Information Processing* (TALIP), 2(2).

Lavie, A., Wintner, S., Eytani, Y., Peterson, E. and Probst, K. 2004. Rapid Prototyping of a Transfer-based Hebrew-to-English Machine Translation System. *Proceedings of the 10th International Conference on Theoretical Methodological Issues in Machine Translation* (TMI-2004).

Lavie, A., Agarwal, A. 2007. METEOR: An Automatic Metric for MT Evaluation with High Levels of Correlation with Human Judgments. *Proceedings of the 2nd Workshop on Statistical Machine Translation at the 45th Meeting of the ACL (ACL-2007),* pp. 228—231.

Lavie, A. 2008. Stat-XFER: A General Search-based Syntax-driven Framework for Machine Translation. Invited paper in Proceedings of CICLing-2008.

Haifa, Israel, February 2008. Gelbuch (ed.), *Computational Linguistics and Intelligent Text Processing*, LNCS 4919, Springer. pp. 362-375.

Palmer, F. 1986. *Mood and Modality*. Cambridge University Press.

Probst, K., Levin, L., Peterson, E., Lavie, A., and Carbonell, J. 2002. MT for Minority Languages Using Elicitation-Based Learning of Syntactic Transfer Rules. Machine Translation, 17 (4).

Quirk, R., Greenbaum, S. 1973. *A University Grammar of English*. Longman.

Williams, E. 1962. *From Latin to Portuguese: Historical Phonology and Morphology of the Portuguese Language*. University of Pennsylvania Press.

Author Index

Association for Computational Linguistics
209 N. Eighth Street
Stroudsburg, Pennsylvania 18360

CURRAN ASSOCIATES INC
proceedings.com